You Can Hear
the Voice of God
CLEARLY

How to go from the still small voice
to the voice of God

By Kevin E. Winters

www.doinglifeonfire.org

Published by Kevin E. Winters, 12700 Denny Court, Upper Marlboro MD
doinglifeonfire@yahoo.com

International Standard Book Number:
978-0-9977334-1-9

Printed in the United States of America

Cover design and page layout by Artiest Design and Illustration

Dedication

I would like to dedicate this book to the most special people I have had the pleasure to know. First I would like to dedicate this to my mother Lynn Rose Winters. Thank you for your effortless and tireless approach to child rearing. Though you are not with us on earth I am very much a product of the wisdom that you spoke to us while you were here.

I would also like to dedicate this to my grandparents DeWanye and Queen Bush who have laid the foundation of a great legacy. This book is proof of that foundation. Thank you for being examples of godliness.

Then there are those in my life that are still on this side of Glory. I would like to dedicate this to my beautiful wife and friend, Tanya and our four children Autumn, Caleb, Aaron, and Noelle. Thank you for sharing me with the world. Thank you for putting up with daddy talking into the air. I am grateful that I have a family that allows me to be me. I love you all with every bit of my person.

Table of Contents

Just A Word

First let me start by saying that this book is for those who have some ability to hear the voice of God. This book will not cover the techniques and mechanics of receiving the voice of God. For complete information regarding how to hear God's voice, the ways He speaks, and how to discern the differences between His voice, your voice, and Satan's voice, you may purchase a copy of my book titled, *"God, Is that You, Me, or the Devil? How to confidently know God's voice."*

That being said, what you will find in the pages of this book is a starting point for your expectation. If you have never heard God's voice, you will learn of some of the reasons why and how to overcome those obstacles. While you may not learn the techniques and mechanics of hearing God's voice in this book you will at least know where to start.

Happy reading!

Kevin E. Winters
CEO, Doing Life On Fire

Preface

Have you ever had the experience of hearing the voice of God clearly at one moment and unclearly in the next moment? Most people have experienced this phenomenon. Have you ever wondered why such a thing occurs? Or have you ever heard anyone speak about the issue of how to hear God's voice clearly? Have you ever considered the fact that you can hear the voice of God clearly and consistently?

I have often looked through the scriptures and wondered how it was that Abraham, Elijah, Paul, and many others heard God's voice. From just reading the Bible it appears that they all heard something so clear that they were never aloof to His instructions for any given situation. It was obvious in the scriptures that they heard with precision and clarity. So how did they hear God's voice with such clarity?

This question arises in me simply because it is so rare to see such a thing in the church today. There is a stark difference between what we see in the relationship of the biblical figures to God and today's men and women of God. It is indeed rare to see Pastors and other church leaders who hear from God with precision and clarity.

This is fascinating to me because the New Testament is the better covenant, but those in the Old Testament had better relationships. This makes me think that we have missed it somewhere.

In the Old Testament God only spoke to certain chosen individuals. These individuals received the coveted title of prophet. In biblical times a prophet was simply a person with whom God chose to speak. But under our new covenant we all have access to God. Hebrews is clear in communicating to us that we can all come before His throne, at any time, in our time of need. This was virtually unheard of under the old covenant. Even among the priest only the High Priest could go into the Holy of Holies. It was in the Holy of Holies that God would appear and speak from between the Mercy Seat. So there was limited access to God under the old covenant. Nonetheless, their experience with the voice of God far exceeds our experience during this era of the church!

For the sake of clarity, let me say that this does not appear to be an Old Testament verses New Testament issue. It appears to be a biblical dispensation verses a post biblical dispensation issue. The Bible records in the book of Acts that the New Testament Church also had grand access to God. In fact I dare say that God intentionally provided the church many stories that indicate that all believers had access to God. For instance visions were not limited to the apostles. This we know because there was a man whom encountered Jesus in a vision who was described as just a "disciple". Many have speculated that he was a prophet, but the Bible is generally clear in its references to who was a prophet in the book of Acts. For example, it says that Barnabas and Silas were prophets. It says that Agabus was a prophet. But when referencing this particular believer it is clear that he was just a disciple. For the average believer this is good news and it does indeed validate the idea that everyone has access to God, unlike those under the old covenant.

As it further relates to us this disciple, we read of a level of access to God's voice that many of us could not fathom. Not only did he see Jesus in a vision but he also conversed with Him in the vision. Try telling someone in the church today that you had a visitation from Jesus. I am more certain that you would be shunned and looked upon with skepticism. You would also be made to feel as if your experience was somehow unbiblical. This tells me that there is a-disconnect between the experiences of the early church and the experiences of the church today.

As for those who dare to hear God's voice today, many of them seem limited to what is called a "still small voice". It is generally described with such phrases as "I feel the Lord saying" or "I believe God said" and is often followed by thoughts of doubt, fear, and uncertainty. Those who hear God's voice today rarely seem as confident as those in the Bible.

Neither do they seem to have precise instructions such as those in the Bible. I believe it all boils down to clarity or the lack thereof.

What if I told you that you could get precise instructions from God? What if I told you that you could hear His voice in a way that is clearer than a "still small voice"? That is what this small book is all about. It is about discovering how to go from uncertainty to certainty, from a faint whisper to a clearly discernable voice. It is about you being able to hear God's voice clearly.

In this book I intend to explore this subject by examining the basis of the still small voice doctrine. Why, you may ask? It all started with a dream; a dream in which God showed me that we could hear Him clearly. Not only did He show me that we could hear clearly, but He also revealed to me how. Last He told me so by opening His word to me and teaching me about this issue. So if you are interested in what He taught me, and if you are interested in experiencing more, then turn the page and discover how "You can hear the voice of God clearly?"

Introduction

For years there has been a standard teaching in the church regarding the voice of God. It is what most would call a landmark teaching and it was one that I wholeheartedly embraced and implemented into my life. It was also all I expected to experience regarding the voice of God. That was until I had a dream many years ago. It was a dream that would shift my paradigm regarding how I would experience hearing the voice of God. It was a dream that would challenge my mindset and push my faith. It was a life changing moment that would lead to an incredible experience with God.

In this landmark dream I was on the phone conversing with a woman. As the dream progressed and our conversation continued, I decided to minister prophetically to her. At that point I started to feel impressions in my spirit and words of knowledge began to flow to my mind. As the words of knowledge began to flow, I started to notice that the deeper I tuned into God, the more audible His voice became. I remember thinking to myself in the dream, "How is this possible?" It was so awesome of an experience that it left a strong impression on my mind upon waking.

At that particular time in my life I was learning how to minister prophetically by faith. So I did not immediately make the connection with what God was really showing me in the dream. I was more excited by God challenging me to step out to minister prophetically by faith. Also the idea of hearing God clearer than a still small voice just seemed too surreal to consider.

However, that would not be the last time that God addressed me about the voice of God and hearing it clearly. It would be later that year as I sat down to write my book, *God, Is that You, Me, or the Devil,* that God would really begin to open me up to this truth.

I remember that day so vividly. I was sitting at my computer working on the chapter that defines the various ways God speaks. I had already written about dreams and visions and I was just starting to write about the "still small voice". As I sat writing about this subject, God suddenly started talking to me about what really happened with Elijah and the still small voice. He started challenging me that we could hear a clearer more discernable voice. Initially I reacted with a sense of wonder. It was the same feeling that I first felt when God presented this idea to me in the dream. I had always been taught that God speaks in a still small. Regardless of the fact that God was telling me differently, I struggled to let go of my old way of thinking. People had taught me an age-old truth, and God was telling me something different. I know that it seems obvious whom I should have believed, but unfortunately I didn't believe God.

I held on to this truth for many years, never sharing it with anyone. I believed it, I could explain it, but I just didn't yield to it. God however, did not give up on me regarding this issue. The next time He spoke to me regarding this issue He did so by presenting it to me in a unique way. One morning as I awoke from sleeping, I heard a song in my heart. There was nothing strange about this experience. In fact it was quite normal. I usually wake up with the sound of faint worship in my heart so I thought nothing of the experience. This time however, I heard a song that I only knew by its melody. Even though I was familiar with the melody I did not know but a few of the lyrics. So in my effort to participate in what God was doing, I "googled" the lyrics, found the song, and downloaded it to my phone. Then I sang along as the day continued. Later in the day I started to notice that the song in my heart was becoming progressively louder. At that moment I felt like Moses when He saw the burning bush. The Bible says that he turned aside at the sight of a burning bush to see why it was not consumed by the fire. Likewise, I also turned aside to see what was happening on the inside of me. As I gave my attention to the song I noticed that the song was loud, distinct, and clear—it was audible. This lasted for two weeks. During that time my days and nights were filled with audible worship. Then it all came to an end and the music I heard in my heart had a new quality. Once it returned to a normal volume level it appeared to be more distant than low in volume. This was all very fascinating to me. This however, was not the end of my experience because something else occurred during the time of audible worship—God spoke to me. And it was just as He had shown me in the dream. The more I tuned in to hear, the clearer His voice became. It seemed audible.

I will never forget that day. It was a precursor to some of my most memorable conversations with God. I have had many conversations and received many insights into life's mysteries. But the most memorable and deep conversations occurred in this season of hearing the voice of God.

While I would like to assume that my experience was unique, that would not be altogether true. This experience is not unique to me it is available to you as well. In fact that is what this book is about. God told me as He spoke to me about this subject, that He was turning up the volume. It has never been His intent for us to stop at hearing the still small voice. The still small voice is a sign of our awakening to the reality that God speaks. Now however, is the time when God's voice will be heard.

The Bible says, "See that you do not refuse Him who speaks" (Heb. 12:25). This passage is clear in communicating that God wants us to hear so that we can obey. How can you refuse Him that speaks if you've never heard Him speak! Or if what you hear is so faint that it's hard to accurately determine what is said. God wants to speak to His people and I am going to fill your heart with that possibility in the pages that follow. God is going to turn up the volume! You can hear the voice of God clearly!

1 | My Sheep Hear My Voice

One of the most common experiences recorded in the scriptures is that of God speaking to people. In fact the Bible is nothing more than a collection of recorded conversations between individuals and God. The other thing that is clearly visible is the fact that God has a voice. This is important to note because there is a teaching that promotes the idea that God speaks in still small voice.

What I am attempting to do in this writing is show you that the still small voice is a starting point to a much clearer hearing experience. If I were to be technical about this subject, I could show you that based on the rules of scripture interpretation, the still small voice theory is not valid at all. Why? It is only mentioned one time in all of scripture. That's right! You never see it mentioned again outside of 1 Kings 19. Second, we see that God speaks in a clear voice hundreds of times throughout scripture.

You may be wondering why I am making this argument. I think that it is imperative for me to make this argument because God has shown me that He wants His people to hear His clear voice. The other reason I am making this argument is based on an experience. In that experience someone told me that I was crazy for thinking that we could hear God's clear voice. This person insisted on holding to the idea that God speaks in a still small voice. This was a clear indication, to me, of our spiritual temperature. It reveals that we are willing to place more faith in one verse of scripture than the hundreds presenting God's clear voice. Likewise I responded to his accusation by simply stating the facts. I said to him, "There are more passages of scripture to justify my point of view than there are to justify yours!"

For this reason, I think that it is plausible to see what the scriptures actually present to us as truth on the subject. It also becomes important because my conflict with this guy validates something that God told me regarding the subject. He said, "My people hear a still small voice because that is what they have been taught to expect". In other words, be it unto to you according to your faith. You can clearly see this at work in the life of this guy with whom I had the encounter. He thought it unimaginable that God would speak to us clearly.

Therefore, even though my main idea for what I am going to share moving forward comes from 1 King 19, I think it is plausible to make a case for hearing the clear voice of God.

In John 10:27, Jesus tells us quite plainly that His sheep hear His voice". In fact as we keep reading He goes on further to say that He calls them each by name. What this communicates to us is the reality that God's voice is clear enough for each of us to have a personal encounter with Him.

You may be thinking, "Wait, I don't see that idea in that passage". But I would like to draw your attention to the fact that Jesus says that He calls them by name. In other words He is saying that I speak to each one of my sheep individually. This also implies that He spends time with each one of His sheep so that they are able to recognize His voice and respond to it. He does not only speak to them collectively and corporately, but as individuals. Last I would like to point out that in order for them to respond they have to each be able to hear a clear voice. There is no confusion in the Master's sheep simply because He treats them as individuals, speaking to each with His own voice.

I Heard a Voice

When reading the Bible you are going to see the phrase "and I heard a voice" or "in a dream a voice said". Each time it is a clearly discernable voice. Peter says in Acts 10:10, I fell into a trance and I heard a voice speaking to me.

I know that this is a hard truth to swallow. This is why it took me so long to embrace it even though God Himself told me twice. The idea that we can actually hear clearly the voice of God seems unimaginable. In fact, I've even been fearful to even share it for fear of people saying, "You are crazy". I still feel this way even though I can clearly prove my point of view in the scriptures.

Speaking of scriptures, let's look at a few passages where the voice of God was absolutely clear.

Moses Exodus 3:4-6

4 So when the Lord saw that he turned aside to look, God called to him from the midst of the bush and said, "Moses, Moses!" And he said, "Here I am." **5** Then He said, "Do not draw near this place. Take your sandals off your feet, for the place where you stand is holy ground." **6** Moreover He said, "I am the God of your father—the God of Abraham, the God of Isaac, and the God of Jacob." And Moses hid his face, for he was afraid to look upon God.

Abemelec Genesis 20:3-7

3 But God came to Abimelech in a dream by night, and said to him, "Indeed you are a dead man because of the woman whom you have taken, for she is a man's wife."**4** But Abimelech had not come near her; and he said, "Lord, will You slay a righteous nation also? **5** Did he not say to me, 'She is my sister'? And she, even she herself said, 'He is my brother.' In the integrity of my heart and innocence of my hands I have done this."**6** And God said to him in a dream, "Yes, I know that you did this in the integrity of your heart. For I also withheld you from sinning against Me; therefore I did not let you touch her. **7** Now therefore, restore the man's wife; for he is a prophet, and he will pray for you and you shall live. But if you do not restore her, know that you shall surely die, you and all who are yours."

Solomon 1 Kings 3: 4-5

4 Now the king went to Gibeon to sacrifice there, for that *was* the great high place: Solomon offered a thousand burnt offerings on that altar. **5** At Gibeon the Lord appeared to Solomon in a dream by night; and God said, "Ask! What shall I give you?"

Phillip Acts 8:29

29 Then the Spirit said unto Philip, Go near, and join thyself to this chariot.

As we read through these passages there is one thing that is presented consistently. That is the truth that people heard the voice of God clearly. Some heard it outwardly while some heard it internally. Regardless of how the voice was received they heard it clear enough to converse with God.

The question then, is why is it thought to be so unimaginable? God says of Himself, "I am God, I do not change" (See Mal. 3:6). If God did not change, we should be willing to open ourselves up for what He did in biblical times. The Bible also says that He shows no partially (See Rom. 2:11). This simply means that what God did then for these great men, He will do for us as well. You can hear God's clear voice!

2 | Conversing with God

Did you know that it is possible to converse with God? This is something else that we do not like to admit is possible. In fact, if you tell someone that you had a conversation with God, they are likely to admit you for mental evaluation. For most people the idea that God dialogs with humans is unimaginable. I know that I am really pushing the boundaries for a lot of those reading. More than likely you just came into the realization that you that you could hear from God. And now I am telling you that you can do more than just hear—you can converse with Him.

This is most evident when reading the books of the prophets. When you look at the scriptures you will see that the prophets had dialog with God. He told them what He was planning to do, and they interacted in conversation with Him. Sometimes the words they heard from Him were so disturbing that they fell on their face to interceded. It is in these moments that we see a naturally flowing conversation between God and man.

One of my favorite examples of this idea is seen in the life of Jonah. The thing that makes it interesting is the way God and the prophet interact at the end of the book when Jonah was angry. The last story is one of the clearest depiction of communion between God and the prophets.

Here's the setup to this idea. God told Jonah to prophesy the destruction of a city called Nineveh. Jonah however decided that he didn't want to do that and he ran in the opposite direction. Eventually he found himself in a divine storm and then in the belly of a whale. In the whale he repented and was spit out onto the shores. Finally he obeyed and the people repented which resulted in God showing mercy and He relented from destroying the city.

This however is quite the problem for Jonah. He had gone through a lot to deliver that word. He got caught in a storm, thrown into the ocean, swallowed by whale, and spit out. After all that he had been through to be obedient he was more than a little disturbed with God. But in his anger we see a hint of relationship in the dialog.

In his anger Jonah sat on a hill overlooking the city and waited to see God destroy Nineveh. As he waited God said to him, "Is it right for you to be angry?" To which Jonah did not reply. So God created a plant to protect him from the sun then allowed it to be destroyed. This allowed the sun's heat to beat on him, which really infuriated him! Then God asked again, "Is it right for you to be angry about the plant?" To which he replied, "It is right for me to be angry, even unto death!" Then God took the time to explain to him why He did not destroy the city. (Jonah 4:1-11)

What makes this awesome to me is the fact that God is not as harsh as we would like to make Him. He took the time to dialog with Jonah and even created an illustration to help the prophet with his emotions. It is almost a parallel to Cain and God's discussion where you see a level of intimacy that allowed them to speak frankly about their feeling with God.

What I want you to take away from this story is the relational dialog that is seen between God and man. It is something that is visible all throughout the Bible from Genesis to Revelations. Men and women dialoged with God!

Look at these passages:

Abraham converses with God Genesis 18:22-33

22 Then the men turned away from there and went toward Sodom, but Abraham still stood before the Lord. **23** And Abraham came near and said, "Would You also destroy the righteous with the wicked? **24** Suppose there were fifty righteous within the city; would You also destroy the place and not spare *it* for the fifty righteous that were in it? **25** Far be it from You to do such a thing as this, to slay the righteous with the wicked, so that the righteous should be as the wicked; far be it from You! Shall not the Judge of all the earth do right?" **26** So the Lord said, "If I find in Sodom fifty righteous within the city, then I will spare all the place for their sakes."**27** Then Abraham answered and said, "Indeed now, I who *am but* dust and ashes have taken it upon myself to speak to the Lord: **28** Suppose there were five less than the fifty righteous; would You destroy all of the city for *lack of* five?" So He said, "If I find there forty-five, I will not destroy *it.*"**29** And he spoke to Him yet again and said, "Suppose there should be forty found there?" So He said, "I will not do *it* for the sake of forty."**30** Then he said, "Let not the Lord be angry, and I will speak: Suppose thirty should be found there?" So He said, "I will not do *it* if I find thirty there."**31** And he said, "Indeed now, I have taken it upon myself to speak to the Lord: Suppose twenty should be found there?" So He said, "I will not destroy *it* for the sake of twenty."**32** Then he said, "Let not the Lord be angry, and I will speak but once more: Suppose ten should be found there?" And He said, "I will not destroy *it* for the sake of ten." **33** So the Lord went His way as soon as He had finished speaking with Abraham; and Abraham returned to his place.

Ananias converses with Jesus

10 Now there was a certain disciple at Damascus named Ananias; and to him the Lord said in a vision, "Ananias." And he said, "Here I am, Lord."**11** So the Lord *said* to him, "Arise and go to the street called Straight, and inquire at the house of Judas for *one* called Saul of Tarsus, for behold, he is praying. **12** And in a vision he has seen a man named Ananias coming in and putting *his* hand on him, so that he might receive his sight." **13** Then Ananias answered, "Lord, I have heard from many about this man, how much harm he has done to Your saints in Jerusalem. **14** And here he has authority from the chief priests to bind all who call on Your name." **15** But the Lord said to him, "Go, for he is a chosen vessel of Mine to bear My name before Gentiles, kings, and the children of Israel. **16** For I will show him how many things he must suffer for My name's sake."

In every one of these passages there is an exchange of ideas between God and man. These are a few out of hundreds of places scattered throughout the scriptures where we see this type of interaction. Some of you may be thinking, "But these are chosen men of God." For this reason I included Ananias. The Bible refers to him as nothing more than a disciple. Hopefully you will be encouraged that even little ole you can converse with God.

This makes me think of the other type of words that people today seem to hear from God. A lot of people in the Church of today have encounters with the voice of God that involve God speaking some random word or phrase then nothing more. Apparently God speaks to them and when they ask questions He refuses to answer them or give them clarity. This is another strange thing to me.

Again, this is something that we do not see this occurring in scriptures. I cannot think of one passage of scripture where God engaged someone in conversation and then refused to give them clarity regarding His instructions. I may be wrong, but I cannot think of any examples of God operating this way. Likewise, God has not shown me otherwise.

Again, am I saying that this is not God at work? No. What I am saying is that it is highly likely that when we hear something from God that we assume that He will not respond to our questions. It is even more likely that maybe we just stopped listening after we thought we received His word.

In a latter chapter I deal with how to keep listening. I also explain what it means when God speaks in such a way that God gets our attention.

Here's an example from my own life of how we can converse with God. In early 2015 God began teaching me about the mind, its role in spiritual life, and how to control it. He had been teaching me that the mind sees. One of the things He taught me was that it was possible to be mentally blind. As the conversation concluded the following occurred.

The conversation went like this:
God: My people are blind
Me: Yeah I know, Lord. They're as blind as a bat!
God: Well, actually a bat sees pretty well.
Me: How so Lord?
God: Bats can see in the dark. Anyone can see in the light. Real vision is being able to see in the dark. That's when seeing is most valuable.
Me: Hummm! That's true.

As you can see from my conversation with the Spirit of God, we can have meaningful dialog with God. This is what He desires. This is just one of my many conversations with God. I could tell you of an occasion that lead to me supernaturally playing the piano. Again, this is what God desires! This is what He died for—the opportunity to converse with mankind again.

This opportunity to dialog with God is something that we struggle to accept as a possibility and a reality. After this particular conversation I took the opportunity to minister it on Facebook. This is something that I do often. As I was sharing the revelation about seeing at night God began to increase the ideas in this truth and it became a full blown message. A friend saw the post and suggested that I leave out the part about my conversation with God and just share the truth I got from it. She was afraid that people were not ready to think that God speaks to people that way. What she was saying was exactly why I shared it. It is unimaginable to people that God dialogs with humans. This only further fueled my passion to share it. I want people to know that it is possible and that will only happen by those who are willing to share the experience.

Furthermore, it is the example He left us in the scriptures. There is nothing that I am saying is possible in your relationship with God that does not exist in the scriptures. We can converse with God!

3 | We Have Senses

Most people do not consider the reality that we have spiritual senses. Hebrews 5:14 tells us that strong food belongs to the mature who have had their "senses" not "sense" exercised to discern good from evil.

Hebrews 5:14

14 But solid food belongs to those who are of full age, *that is,* those who by reason of use have their senses exercised to discern both good and evil.

Jesus likewise suggests that we have spiritual senses when He points that we have issues with our "eyes" and "ears".

Matthew 13:15

15 For the hearts of this people have grown dull. Their ears are hard of hearing, And their eyes they have closed, Lest they should see with their eyes and hear with their ears, Lest they should understand with their hearts and turn, So that I should heal them.'

Most of us focus on developing just the sense that God exposes to us first. Therefore, we have people today that call themselves seers (chozen) and others who call themselves hearers (nabi). This distinction is operation generally causes us to cease developing our other senses.

A lot of people understand what it is to "feel" the voice of God. It is probably the most common experience of all. It is perception at work. The Bible says "Jesus perceived in His spirit…" (Mark 2:8) Paul said "Men I perceive…"(Act 27:10). This is our sense of feeling in our spirit.

Some of us "see" in the spirit. Again this is a common experience for a lot of people. In fact the Bible is full of dreams and visions. Some estimate that dreams and visions account for two-thirds of all communication between God and mankind. This has led to the idea that this is the primary way that God speaks. Likewise it has led to a healthy, and sometimes unhealthy, fascination with dreams and visions. I say unhealthy because Numbers 12:6 however, is clear that God would rather speak to us by His voice face to face.

Last, there is our sense of "hearing". This is also seen in multiple places in the Bible but is rarely seen today. In fact it is so rare that it is considered to be an awe-inspiring experience. Most of us have become accustomed to "feeling" and "seeing" and we have neglected to develop our last sense— Our spiritual ears.

When I first started hearing the voice of God I experienced Him in all three ways. I felt the voice speaking to me. I heard a clear voice speaking. And I saw His voice in dreams and visions. While these are all valid ways that we hear, they are all distinct ways that we experience God through our various spiritual senses.

Over time God initiated a process to develop each sense in me separately. The first sense upon which He concentrated developing was my sense of feeling. During this development phase He only spoke to me through the sense that He was maturing at that time. It all started with a principle, then He would work that idea into my life.

At first, this was very difficult to understand. All of a sudden I went from having three senses to depending on one. For years God did not speak to me by His voice or by dreams and visions. He only spoke by perception. He only made an exception on two occasions that I can remember. One occurred when I became entangled in legal trouble regarding a client's book. I am a graphic designer by trade. As such, I took the responsibility of laying out the content and designing the cover for my client's book. The problem we encountered occurred because I assumed more responsibility than I had time to commit to. Obviously this was not a good equation and I went far beyond the contracted deadline. Being understandably angry, my client threatened me with a lawsuit for breech of contract.

All of a sudden I was facing a lawsuit and she wanted her money returned. But I had already spent it. She was very angry to say the least. Immediately I sought to hear from God and turned to perception for the answer. To my surprise, I encountered the voice of God. At this point, I had not heard His voice in over 3 or 4 years. I was relieved to hear from Him in this situation. My heart was filled with fear and I did not know what to do. As I sought the Lord He said, "She'll be fine. Finish the book!" So even though my customer was furious, and I did not have permission to proceed with the book, I followed God's instructions and finished the project.

The following day or so I presented the completed product to my client. She went from ballistic to overjoyed and she was very impressed by my work. Not only did she continue on with me in this project, but we have completed many other projects together.

The next spiritual sense upon which God would focus His efforts were my spiritual ears. Only this time He did not cease communicating with me through perception. Instead He encouraged me to use what He had taught me about perception to measure the voice of God. What you are reading is the product of my development process.

The last spiritual sense up for development was my spiritual eyes. This has all been very interesting. Before I had any understanding of what was happening, I just flowed with whatever God was doing. Now, however, understanding has made me fully aware of everything that is happening. We are still in the process of fine-tuning my eyes even as I am writing this book. Maybe I will write on the subject of spiritual eyes at a latter time.

The goal of this chapter is to help each person realize that it is not the intent of God that we focus on developing just one of our senses. For instance, if during an examination with your primary care physician it was discovered that you could hear but could not see, or that you could see but could not hear, you would be classified as handicapped. Well, there is no difference when we consider the spiritual significance of this scenario. God expects us to use and develop our "senses" not our "sense".

This has practical applications. Let's look at this from the natural. Ears and eyes are designed to optimize our ability to communicate. Ears allow us to hear sounds and interpret their meanings to those who understand the language. Eyes are used to interpret the symbols seen and relay meaning to the brain. For instance when we see a person with a yellow umbrella we are presented with a symbol of something to be communicated. Based on the position of the umbrella we make certain judgements. If it is down we may assume that it is going to rain. If it is up we may assume that it is raining. So our sight is a part of our communication system.

Spiritually speaking, the same is true with our spiritual eyes. Try to imagine God effectively communicating to Abraham the magnitude of his seed with mere words. Remember He took Abraham outside the tent and had him to look up at the sky and told him that his descendants would be as numerous as the stars in the sky. Again, try to imagine this concept without a visual. The impact is immediately lessened by the lack of a visual. This means that there are some things that we hear that are better understood seen.

Another example is found in the entirety of the book of Zachariah. Zachariah is one of the most visionary rich book books in the Bible. As you read it you are left in awe at the level of visions he received. But try to imagine God using only words to describe this whole book. Try to imagine John hearing the book or revelations. I'm sure that you will agree that it sounds ridiculous. Likewise it sounds ridiculous that one would expect balance from only seeing or only hearing the voice of God. You need both!

Over the years God has raised up people such as Bill Hamon to teach us how to feel. I once saw an interview with Bill where he shared how he begged God to let him see what was coming before he prophesied. He said that God told him do it the way He designed him. Now this may appear contradictory. The truth is that God designed Bill for a purpose that was much larger than what he could perceive. God has used him to help people develop their prophetic sense of feeling.

God has likewise has raised up many people who are "seers" only. He has also trained them in that aspect of spiritual communication. He allowed them to specialize in a particular form of spiritual communication because He needed them to train others to see.

Now, however, is the time when God is revealing to us that we need to cross train. In fact we see this happening more today than ever. We see seers that hear as well as hearers that see. This is God at work teaching us to develop our senses.

God has made me neither a seer nor a hearer. I can now operate in all three of my senses. I can hear the clear distinct voice of God. I can see in dreams and visions. Last, I can feel or perceive what God is saying to me and what's happening in the spiritual world around me.

I encourage you to develop all three. Even though I took the time in this chapter to deal with all three of these senses, please keep in mind that this book is only about our sense of "hearing". There has been much teaching to develop "feelers" and "seers". Now is the time that God is developing the "hearers".

4 | Spiritual Ears

Concerning hearing the voice of God, let me start by saying, there are two distinct ways that the audible voice of God is heard in the Bible. There is an external voice, such as that heard by Moses. There is also, and internal audible voice. We see these two examples in scripture. One occurs in the life of Peter in his vision on the rooftop. The other occurs in the life of Ananias when Jesus spoke to him regarding the Apostle Paul. When I say we can hear the clear voice of God, I am referring to an internal audible voice.

I am sure that some of you think that I'm referring to what we hear with our natural ears. However, I am referring to what we hear with our spiritual ears. In Job 33:14-15 one of Job's friends makes a declaration that God often speaks to us in dreams at night because we are insensitive to His voice during our waking hours. One of the interesting things he said was that **"God opens man's ears"** at night. The ears he is referring to are our spiritual ears. This is an important distinction to make, because the way our physical ears interpret sound does not equate to how your spiritual ears interpret sound. For instance, Daniel says in his experience with an angel, "And I heard the sound of his words…" (See Dan. 10:9) He did not say the sound of his voice, but the sound of His words. The same happens when we hear the voice of God. You are not necessarily going to hear a voice with pitch and tone, though it may appear that way. You will hear the sound of His words. The truth is that there in little difference when compared to hearing a song in your head. Even though you may hear what you think are musical notes, or a voice singing. You are not really hearing in the natural sense of the word. You are perceiving the sounds as they appear as impressions in the mind. The same is true with the voice of God. You will feel the sound of His voice and it may even appear to have pitch and tone. I have heard it as a gentle man's voice. In fact, I have heard is so clearly at times preaching to me, that I do little more than open my mouth and repeat what I heard. It can be that clear!

One reality we must acknowledge is the fact that we have outward senses and inner senses. As it relates to our natural senses, we already know that our physical ears allow us to hear sounds such as cars, voices, music, etc. What we never really consider however, is the fact that you have ears that hear inwardly as well. Your inner ears hear the sounds of your heart. With these hidden ears we hear our thoughts and inner voice. Likewise, unknown to us we also hear God and demons as well. God's voice is generally easy to hear because His word burns in our heart. I have found that the most common problem for most Christians is not hearing God's voice it is distinguishing His voice from ours. The same is true with demons. Most people do not realize that some of the ideas and ranting that they hear inwardly is a demon of some type.

Another way we know that we have inner ears is because God said to Miriam and Aaron in Numbers 12:6 "If there is a prophet among you I speak to him **in** a dream, I speak to him **in** a vision". Notice that God does not say that He is speaking to the prophet **"by"** a dream and vision, but **in** a dream and vision. That word **"in"** is critical to our understanding because it tells us that there is a part of us that hears spiritual beings. It likewise conveys to us that our "inward" part is what we use to make contact in with the spiritual realm. When you think about it, it makes sense. Jesus said, God is a Spirit and we worship Him in spirit and truth (John 4:24).

Notice in the scriptures, especially in Daniel, how the prophet is conversing with an angel, a spiritual being. And he is doing so in a dream. Dreams occur inwardly. It was in the dream that he heard the angel's voice. You will also notice this reality in the many dreams in the Bible. Then as a personal example, you can attest to the reality that your dreams have "sound"! So there is a part of us that hears the physical world around us and a part of our human design that hears the invisible world around us as well. This is all possible due to our spiritual ears—ears which we all possess.

5 | The Story that Started it All

Where did this idea of a still small voice originate? Anyone who has ever read a book or attended a teaching session on the subject of the voice of God has heard that God speaks in a still small voice. This idea of the "still small voice" is derived from a famous story in 1 Kings 19. It is the story of one of the most powerful demonstration of a man operating under God's power. It is such an awe-inspiring story that the man God used to do this unimaginable miracle is often regarded as a biblical legend. His name was Elijah. He did such things as call for a drought and declared that it would not rain except at his word. And it happened just as he said. We also read of him calling down fire from heaven on two occasions. But the miracle that made him a legend occurred when this prophet challenged the king's false prophets to a showdown of the gods.

In this showdown he challenged the false prophets to call on their god while he called on the Lord. The point was that the God that answered by fire would be God. Of course, they were not able to produce any results. God however, showed up and demonstrated His awesomeness. He made it absolutely clear to all that were present that He and He alone is God.

What an exciting miracle. The false prophets were killed by the people as God returned their hearts to Himself. All seemed to be going well. Then the queen sent Elijah a message. She wrote in her letter to Elijah that he would be dead by the next day. This struck fear into the heart of this great prophet and he ran into the desert ready to die. While there an angel gave him instructions to keep moving. Elijah however went into a cave. It was what happened to Elijah in the cave that established the doctrine of the still small voice.

In order to see what really happened we must take notice of three distinct terms used to describe Elijah's experience with the voice of God. They are "the word of the Lord", verse 9, "a still small voice", verse 12, and "a sudden voice", verse 13. (See 1 Kings 19:9-13)

In this passage we are presented with a scared and tired Elijah who was sitting in a cave still overwhelmed by the threat against his life from Queen Jezebel. While he was in hiding he suddenly came into an awareness of God speaking to him. This can be described as perception or it may have been by a dream. Numbers 12:6-8 tells us that if God speaks to a prophet He does so in dreams and visions. Therefore it is highly likely that this occurred in a dream. The other indication that this is a possibility is the fact that we know that Elijah fell asleep in the cave. During this initial encounter God questioned him regarding why he was in the cave. At that time God also instructed him to go to the entrance of the cave (1 Kings 19:11). Elijah however, remained where he was. Everything else that followed happened on the heels of this information.

While Elijah was still in the cave the Lord passed by and Elijah saw at the entrance various experiences. One of these experiences was described as "a still small voice" (verse 12). It was at that moment that Elijah obeyed God's initial instructions and went to the front of the cave (verse 13). Upon arriving at the place he was initially commanded to be, he heard a clear voice whose content was identical to the "word of the Lord" which came to him in the cave.

What I am hoping is evident is the progression within the story. One, Elijah perceived that he needed to go to the front of the cave. Two, God said something that could only be described as a whisper. And three, as Elijah got closer to where was supposed to be, he realized that God speaking to him. While this passage has been a base teaching for years regarding hearing the voice of God, you will notice that the still small voice is an attribute of few conditions—conditions that we will discuss moving forward. You will also notice that the whisper has no clarity, but the "sudden" voice does.

So when you read the actual text that promotes the idea of the still small voice, you will see that Elijah did not hear the voice of God clearly until he heard what the scripture says was a "sudden voice".

Does that mean that people hearing a still small voice are hearing some other voice. No! What it means is that they, like myself, have come to expect what they were taught.

One thing about hearing God's voice that we must come to realize is that it is done by faith. In fact the writer of Hebrews tells us to prophesy (speak what we hear from God) by faith. This means that faith is a vital part of our being able to receive more from God. Likewise, the book of James says if you lack wisdom and you need to hear from God do so in faith or you will not be able to receive God's answer. I will deal with this in more detail in a latter section.

So what was the role of the still small voice in the passage? That among other questions is what I intend to answer going forward.

6 | Why Elijah Heard God Whispering-
Disobedience

In the last chapter we dissected 1 Kings 19 to see what really happened in that passage. One thing that I hope was very evident is the fact that the still small voice was not the voice that Elijah dialoged with. Yes, he heard a still small voice, but it was not intended to describe God's voice in the experience. The other thing that I want you to take away from the last chapter is the fact that the still small voice was the beginning of what led to a clear voice. If the clear voice of God is what He desires, then we must explore the passage to discover why Elijah heard a still small voice.

So why did Elijah hear a whispering voice. There are four things in the passage that led to the whisper. They are:

1. Disobedience
2. A lack of Focus
3. Spiritual Warfare
4. Pain

Disobedience

One of the things most evident in the passage is Elijah's disobedience. God had instructed him to go to the entrance of the cave (verse 9). Then God Himself went to the entrance of the cave. But upon His divine appearance guess who was not there when He started speaking. You may be saying to yourself, I don't see his disobedience in the text. But there are some key indicators that tell us this much is true.

One, verse 13 says that Elijah did not come out of the cave until he heard the still small voice. It says, "So it was when Elijah heard it, he wrapped his face in his mantle and came out." Two, we must consider, that between God's initial instruction to go to the entrance of the cave and the moment Elijah heard the still small voice, some events occurred. Those events occurred in verse 12. It says that there was an earthquake, a fire, and a wind that tore into the mountains breaking the rocks in pieces. What this tells us is that there was a passing of time between the initial instruction and Elijah choice to obey.

This means that God moved on from that place and Elijah had not. And it was his disobedience that led to a physical distance between where he was and were God was at the time that He started speaking. The distance led to the voice of God appearing as a faint whisper.

Here is an example I like to use whenever I teach on this subject. On my honeymoon my wife and I decided that we were going to rent jet skis. I had never been on one before so I was a little excited to say the least. When we got on the jet ski our instructor immediately pointed to cones that marked the boundaries in the ocean. He said very clearly that we were not to exceed the boundary. So we nodded in agreement to those terms and we started riding. We were having so much fun. Approximately half way through the rental time I got an idea to go beyond the boundaries. So I did. There I was outside of the established boundary having a blast. Finally I decided to turn around and head inland. Just as we were approaching the cone marking the boundary the jet ski ran out of gas. I cannot describe the feeling of helplessness that came over me that day. Here I was stuck in the middle of the ocean with my new bride, who by the way tried to warn me not to break the boundary. As we sat there helpless we started screaming for help. Even though we were beyond the boundary we were close enough to see the instructor on the shore. So we screamed for help. The problem we encountered became real when we realized that our vision traveled further than our sound. We were close enough to be seen but not close enough to be heard. The physical distance between us and the instructor had minimized the impact of our voice. Likewise the only reason we were distant was because we were disobedient!

The same happened in Elijah's experience. His disobedience put a distance between he and God. And that distant literally impacted and reduced the sound of God's voice to a whisper.

There is no doubt in my mind that someone reading this is saying to themselves, "How can a person be distant from God." However, I would like to point out to you that James says that we are to "Draw near to God and He will draw near to us" (James 4:8). I would like you to consider that if we can draw near to God, then it is possible to be distant. In Isaiah 59:2, the prophet echoes this idea. It says, "But your iniquities have separated you from your God; And your sins have hidden His face from you, so that He will not hear"

Many times we underestimate the damage that disobedience and sin has on our relationship with God. This happens to all of us. We all go through seasons or situations when the voice of God seems unclear to us. I used to say, God why are you so quiet? I would ask this question whenever His voice seemed faint and hard to detect. Then He taught me the truth in Elijah's experience and now I can identify what is happening. Whenever the voice of God is unclear in your life you may be in a place of disobedience. Just like in Elijah's experience, when we are is a place of disobedience we are akin to being distant from where God wants us to be and likewise, His voice seems distant.

Now let me acknowledge that I do not believe that Elijah was sinning. He was distressed and it is possible that his obedience was delayed due to the condition of his state of mind at that time. That being said, there are however, times when sin comes between us and God. But it should be noted that the issue is never with God, it is always with us. Sin stains the conscience and for that reason many people allow sin to halt their efforts to press into God. Whatever you do don't allow sin to force you out, but use repentance to press in! It is in the presence of God that we find deliverance from the power of sin. But either way, whether the distance between you and God is created by sin or disobedience, just know that you can be distant from God relationally.

For me this sometimes seems like a constant reality check. I have come to a place where hearing God clearly has become normal. That being the case, I more readily realize that when His voice seems distant or low in volume, that I am out of compliance with something He wants me to do.

As it relates to disobedience people are generally aware of the fact that they are out of compliance with God's instructions. An example from my life comes from a time when God was teaching me healing. He had been teaching me about how to minster healing more effectively. As He did His voice was absolutely clear. After a while He began challenging me to apply what He taught me.

For me the challenge was not trusting God to heal the sick. I knew that He was healer because He once healed me. My problem stemmed from my inability to reach out to strangers. I thought to myself, these people are going to think I'm crazy. I also wondered, what I would say to introduce myself. Either way, God had given me clear instructions to heal the sick.

After a while I did step out in obedience to His command. It was a sometimes "hit" and "miss" type of situation. Sometimes people were healed, sometimes they were not. After a while I became discouraged with the inconsistencies in the manifestation of healings. So I gradually ceased from even attempting to heal the sick. Then gradually over time I began to realize that God was somewhat silent. I did not immediately put two and two together, but eventually I figured out that it was my disobedience.

I cannot speak for everyone, but as it relates to me, my relationship with God is everything. He is the first person I address every morning when I awaken. I generally speak to Him all day about someone or something. He is a very important part of my daily life. So any hindrance to my fellowship with Him is a very real problem.

Upon realizing that I was using passive aggressive behavior to be disobedient, I purposed to resume praying for the sick. As soon as I made up my mind to obey God's initial instructions to me things became clear again.

This is one story, but I could tell you of other instances where my disobedience dimmed God's voice in my life. Likewise, I am certain that as you read this the Holy Spirit is bringing to your mind when your disobedience dimmed His voice in your life as well.

7 | Why Elijah Heard God Whispering-
Lack of Focus

The next thing that has the potential to limit your interaction with God to a whisper is a lack of focus. This is something that we sometimes do not consider. The voice of God is clear to those who learn the value of focus. Elijah's experience with the still small voice is symptomatic of his depression and self-absorption—he became self-centered.

The good attribute of the still small voice is that it calls us to a deeper focus. It was the still small voice that made Elijah explore and look deeper into what the whisper was actually saying. For it reads, "...and when he heard it he wrapped his face in his mantle and **came out**".

So many times we miss God because we are not willing to take the necessary steps to get closer to His voice. We have become satisfied with a whisper. The whisper is a call to keep looking deeper. You will find that this truth also applies to our spiritual eyes. Many prophetic people can attest to the reality of God using a faint image that became clearer and more focused as they kept looking. You will likewise see this in many visionary experiences in the Bible. Many of the prophets said such things as "as I was looking" or "I kept looking". What they were saying was that as they gave more attention to what they were seeing they were able to see more revelation. This truth likewise applies to hearing God's voice.

Elijah recognized the prompting of God, got up from his place, and dared to walk closer to God's voice. Moses does the same. He saw bush burning with fire but it did not burn. Then it says that he turned aside to see why the bush was not burning. As he got closer to what God used to get his attention. He heard a clear voice speak to him.

The key to hearing the clear voice of God can be summed up in Colossians 3:20, set your mind on things above, not on things of the earth. In other words tune in to the right channel. Focus!

Being Deterred

Being in focus also means being in the will God. One thing we see in the story is that Elijah allowed fear and intimidation to deter him from the will of God. For God says to him in 1 Kings 19:9, "What are you doing here Elijah?" The question implies that Elijah is in a place in life other than where God intended.

In fact it seems like a strange question for God to ask a man who was discouraged and suicidal. Nonetheless, God had a legitimate reason for asking the question. In 1 Kings 19:7 an angel appeared to Elijah and said to him "Arise and eat for the journey is great." The word journey is a key word in the verse. It tells us that Elijah had an appointment elsewhere—one that God had obviously appointed. Therefore, God asked him, "Elijah, what are you doing **here**?" Elijah had been deterred from the plan of God.

Determent is different than disobedience. In the last chapter we discussed how Elijah's disobedience to God's instructions positioned him to hear God whispering. Determent however differs because it can be very unintentional. Sometimes we miss God and that's okay. The story teaches us that God's question is an attempt to guide Elijah back into the place He intended. God recognized that Elijah had a life hiccup that detoured his life and He wanted to get him back on track.

We do however, have to acknowledge that it was Elijah's life detour that led to the whisper in the first place. You should know that just as God sought to readjust Elijah's destiny, He will likewise readjust yours. You only need to come closer to the voice when God whispers to get your attention. This is what Elijah did and God put his life back on the proper course.

As we consider the possible meanings for being out of focus, we can narrow it down to one word—distraction! Overall, a lack of focus simply means we are distracted. It is being distracted in prayer— distracted with life—and sometimes distractions can lead to a distracted sense of purpose.

Causes of Distractions

When we look at Elijah's story we see that a distracted lifestyle has a cause. 1 Kings 19 presents us with these causes. They are:

1. Circumstantial position changes
2. Emotional position changes
3. Physical position changes
4. Geographical position changes

Circumstances

The first position change occurs in Elijah's circumstance. In chapter 18 he is seen challenging the false prophets of Baal and calling down fire from heaven. From the standpoint of life he is at the apex of his ministry, anointing, and life. He is triumphantly handling life and just reading about his life in this chapter is very inspiring. Then something happens.

On the heels of this great victory a letter soon follows. In the letter the king's wife threatens the great man of God with death as an exchange for the life of her prophets. All of a sudden he goes from being the victor to being the victim. His circumstances have changed!

37

Emotions

Upon the receipt of the threatening letter the man of God became fearful. So get the picture. Just one chapter previous he was on top of the world. He had challenged 400 prophets by himself, challenged the king, and won the hearts of the people. He was brave just one chapter ago. Now he is afraid for his life.

Physical

All of this leads to another type of change in the passage. The change in his circumstances led the changes in his emotions. These changes led to physical changes in his position. 1 King 19:2-3 says that upon receiving the letter from the queen that he experienced three physical changes. It says that he 1) **ran** in fear, 2) **sat** under a broom tree, 3) **lay** under a broom tree, and 4) **slept** under a broom tree. Each position change was a sign of a declining emotional and mental state. He went from running, to sitting, to lying, finally to sleeping! With each step he got lower and slower.He was declining physically and it is our first sign that something is really wrong. It is a picture of the cycle of depression! As you can see there is something happening in this text that leads to the still small voice.

Geographical

The last thing that I will point out in the passage is that Elijah experiences geographical position changes. He starts in the high place of Mount Carmel, then moves to the wilderness, then finally into a dark cave.

All of these were the foundation of what caused Elijah to become distracted. This all leads to a vital truth. We must be careful in how we handle stressful situations. It was one stressful event that started a process that caused Elijah to change his position. It was his response to the circumstance that led to the emotions of fear. It was the fear that inspired him to run, sit, lie, and sleep. And it was the physical changes that repositioned him from the light into a deep place in a dark cave.

So let's be careful in how we handle the circumstances and challenges in our life. The last thing that I want you to know is that even though Elijah allowed life to drive him into a dark place. It did not drive him into a place beyond the reach of God. He may have heard an unclear voice, but he heard it well enough that it led him into the light where the clear voice of God was speaking. And if you have found yourself in this kind of place, God will get his voice to you too!

8 | Why Elijah Heard God Whispering-
Spiritual Warfare

The next thing that led to the encounter with the still small voice was the least obvious of the four—spiritual warfare. Spiritual warfare is one of the most complicated ideas to get believers to accept. Somehow we know that there is a devil, but we underestimate how involved he is in the world and how committed he is to his job.

We don't see him in the passage but he is there in the person of Queen Jezebel. To really understand my point I must remind you that the only reason Elijah was in a position to hear a still small voice was because of Jezebel's threat. Her threat filled his heart with fear, sent him into depression, and forced him into hiding.

If we are not careful, spiritual warfare can have the same negative impact on our relationship with God and even our ministry. So many people of God have unwittingly gone into hiding because of things happening in their lives. This happens because most people do not realize that Satan's true goal is the same as it has always been—to get you out of fellowship with God. Likewise, he uses circumstances to start the process. Looking at what happened in Genesis chapter 3 we can see that Satan's goal in tempting Adam and Eve was to damage their relationship with God. This damage was intended to extend to the subsequent generations. If we did a study I could show you how over time mankind went from hearing the clear voice of God to a time when they didn't even recognize God speaking to them in the person of Jesus.

This is what every natural negative event Satan inspires is meant to accomplish. He wants to use life's challenges as distractions. Even in the story of Peter walking on the water to Jesus, we can see that it was the winds and waves that distracted him from the word he heard from God. As I said in the last chapter, if we are not careful to handle the challenges of life properly, we run the risk of diminishing our ability to perceive His voice in our lives.

We see the clearest depiction of spiritual warfare against our senses in 1 Kings 6:8-17. The prophet Elisha had been revealing the of king Syria's plan to attack Israel. The king's response was to take the eyes and ears of God from Israel. From a natural standpoint it appeared that this was an exclusively natural situation. Then Elisha prayed for his servant's spiritual eyes to open and he saw something interesting. He saw that there were more angles than demons. Most people don't realize this but Elisha said in verse 16, "**those** who are **with us** are more than **those** who are **with them**". If those with us refer to the angels with the men of God, then who were those with the army? I submit to you that Satan came after the eyes and ears of God.

I can guarantee that this happens to you too. Just when you hear the voice of the Lord speaking, the phone rings, challenges occur, depression kicks in, etc. The same happened to Elijah. He had a monumental victory and it was followed by a threat. Then life happened and his focus shifted from God to self. This is also what Satan did to Adam and Eve. He used life to make them self-centered.

I shall never forget how I learned this principle. I had been enjoying my experience of dialoging with God about various issues. During this time He had instructed me to start a preaching ministry on social media. So I did. Every week He spoke to me to give me instructions and answered questions in preparation of my YouTube and Facebook video posts. All was going fine for the first few weeks of posting. Eventually God began speaking to me about the subject of spiritual warfare. So I taught most of the insights He shared with me on the subject. Up until this point I was still having a very pleasant experience with God. Then I obviously revealed something that hell did not appreciate. Therefore, a demon manifested himself to me at the conclusion of the two week teaching. He had the presence of a principality, or at least that is the impression I got from him. He said something to me that I will not repeat and then attempted to overthrow me to prove he was more powerful. But of course, it did not work because I had fresh revelation regarding how to deal with spiritual warfare so I stood on God's revealed truth. Even though his attempt to overpower me did not work, an intense season of warfare ensued thereafter.

Over the next couple of weeks I began noticing that the voice of God was hard to detect. In fact, God resorted to singing various songs to inspire my next couples of topics. On one occasion he sang to me an old hymn *"Everything to God in Prayer"*. This went on for a "months". It was fascinating, incredible, and annoying to me all at the same time. It fascinated me to see just how much it disturbed Satan that I was dialoging with God. He pulled no punches in his attempts to silence God's voice in my life.

We see a more distinct picture of this type of warfare in Daniel 10:12-13. In this passage of text, Daniel was in prayer regarding a disturbing vision he saw. While in prayer an angel appeared before him with a word from God. Then the angel said an interesting thing. He said that from the time Daniel set his face to understand the vision that God had sent out the answer. Then the angel proceeded to share with him that the word he brought from heaven for Daniel had been resisted. It had been resisted to the point that even though God spoke an answer, it took the angel 21 days—nearly a month, to deliver it.

The angel did not stop there. He went on to share with Daniel that his delay was directly related to a war with territorial spirits (See verse 13). If Daniel endured seasons of warfare that hindered his ability to hear from God then you should expect the same.

However, just know that it is only for a season. For this reason I implore you to learn how to do spiritual warfare. Last I encourage you develop all of your senses. You never know when one of them may come under attack. Even though my hearing and vision was dulled by warfare, I was still able to "feel" the voice of God for direction.

Understanding the Goal of Spiritual Warfare

I feel that it is necessary to really look at this idea of why we need to do spiritual warfare. If hearing the voice of God clearly is our goal, what might you think the opposite of that would be? I would like to re-submit to you that Satan uses distractions to keep us out of focus!

I know that we already discussed focus, but I want you know how spiritual warfare affects our focus. Most people do not consider the idea of the secret place in Psalm 91. It says that there is safety in the secret place. However there is a condition attached to that text. I remind you that it says, "He that dwells in the secret place shall abide in the presence of God." (Pam. 91:1) Notice that the condition is that we "dwell"! Most Christians have learned how to visit the secret place.

So in the morning and just before bed many people practice quieting down their souls so that they can hear from God. This means that during the day most people do not or are not aware of His ever present reality. I have come to eliminate from my vocabulary such phrases as "come Holy Spirit" "God is coming" and "God is here". Why? David said Oh God where could I go from your presence. If I make my bed in the stars You are there. If I travel to the bottom of the ocean you are there..." The principle of the passage is that God is ever present. We never have to conjure Him up. He is always present with us. In fact Jesus said I will be in you and with you always even until the end of the age (Matt. 28:20). This means that we must learn how to practice the presence of God.

Practicing the presence of God means that we allow ourselves to accept the reality of God's ever present presence. It is a willful effort to make ourselves aware of Him.

What does this have to do with spiritual warfare? Part of the battle in regards to spiritual warfare is simply to keep you out of the secret place. Satan does not want you to focus on God because focus leads to a clearer hearing experience. And that leads to his defeat in your life as well as the lives of others.

I am constantly working to master the art of maintaining access to the secret place. I am much further along than I have ever been and I look forward to mastery of it. This means that my mind is quiet most of the time. When God first taught me what I am about to teach you I found myself in an uncomfortable peaceful place. I know that sounds contrary, but that is how I would describe it.

For many of us a noisy mind is considered to be a normal experience. It is unconceivable for many that their days and nights do not have to be filled with worry, fear, anxiety, stress, anger, and such. But God had taught me how to dwell with Him and for the first time I had an absolutely quiet mind. Until that point I was the kind of person that was always thinking about something. This new place in God therefore posed quite the dilemma. I didn't know how to handle it and at first I didn't even like it. I felt like I was in a room all by myself, literally, that is how I felt. It was a wonderfully peaceful place but I missed my noisy mind. Isn't it amazing how we can become comfortable with less than God's best for us?

The best part of this however, it that God's voice did not have to compete with another voices. This meant that I heard Him absolutely clear!

So what did God teach me that made this possible? He showed me that all demonic activity and attacks are rooted in tactics of distraction. For instance, Satan is not after your money, cars, marriage, children, health etc. These things mean nothing to him. He is only after one thing. Your peace of mind! He is after shifting your focus and he uses circumstances to do it.

Here is a biblical example of this idea at work. In the book of Job, chapters 1 and 2, Satan and God have a discussion at which time they both make their ideas about Job known. God says that Job is a man of integrity and honor (Job 1:8). That is God's perspective on Job. Satan offers his idea as well. He says that if certain things in Job's life are removed that Job would curse God and die (verse 11). Cursing God is Satan's agenda. Both God and Satan are at war for the mind of Job. Job's perspective is God's perspective. This is revealed in Job 2:1-22 when upon losing all of his worldly possessions to include his children he says, "From dust we came and from dust we shall return. God has given and God takes away." Job is holding fast to his integrity just as God had said. This was Job's mindset—a mindset Satan wants to shift.

Then Job's wife expresses her mind on the issue after Satan attacks Job's health. Her words to her husband are such, "Do you still hold fast to your integrity. Curse God and die" (Job 2:9) Her words "curse God" are aligned with Satan idea for Job. Then in verse 4 Job's friends show up to comfort him. They were doing a good job until one of them had a dream in which a spirit inspired a conversation that tormented Job for 30 plus chapters. Initially it seemed as though this was a random spirit. That is until we read Job 42:7 in which God confronts Eliphaz, the recipient of the strange dream encounter. God told him that what he and Job's friends said about Him were not right.

So I want you to catch what is happening in the book of Job. Satan has an idea that he is trying to get Job to embrace. But Job has a rock solid idea that protects his perspective of who God is. In an effort to break Job down He used every possible circumstance to position Job's mind to accept the idea that he wanted to plant in him. He killed his children and destroyed his possessions, he attacked his body with vicious boils, he harassed him with nightmares, and he turned Job's friends against him. And all of this was done with the intent of shifting Job's focus.

Spiritual warfare is all about mind warfare. Satan spent a great deal of effort manipulating the physical world around Job and it was all to make him trade the truth for the lie. Since God has taught me this truth I know how to best respond to natural circumstances. The ability to respond correctly also protects your focus. That means a better focus equals a clearer reception of God's voice.

So remember, when life happens again don't fall for the trap. Challenges mean that Satan is trying to start a conversation and fill your mind with unnecessary voices. He is trying to distract you from keeping your mind on Jesus. He does this because he knows that if your mind is focused and clear that you will be able to hear God clear enough to divert his evil plan.

9 | Why Elijah Heard God Whispering-
Pain

The last subject that I want to cover under the subject of why the prophet heard a still small voice is pain. Pain can position us for a still small voice. Pain is dangerous because if left unattended it can harden the heart. Elijah, as we've discussed in the last couple of chapters, is likewise is pain when he hears God whispering. Pain is often the result of spiritual warfare.

We can see pain at work in the life of the Gadarene demoniac (Luke 8:26-39). This story also reveals to us how pain can keep us from hearing God's voice clearly. In the story Jesus is seen speaking to a man whose spiritual problem kept him from hearing God's voice. This symbolizes the hardness of the heart.

A hardened heart is one that is guarded or shielded from being exposed to potential pain. God shared with me an interesting thing. He showed me that the nakedness of mankind in the garden is a depiction of transparency. Initially mankind was transparent in their relationship with God. This means that they felt comfortable enough in their own skin to be who there were on the inside. It was not until sin entered into the world that we see a hardening of man's heart. It is first depicted in

Adam and Eve's attempt to cover themselves from each other. The hiding of their nakedness from each other is the start of a decaying sense of transparency. In doing so they likewise covered themselves from God. This is very significant because they used leaves to hide from each other, but a bush to hide from God. The spiritual significance of this is that we are allowed to see how a natural act of hiding has a major impact spiritually. It is impossible to hide from man without hiding from God. 1 John 4:20 says, "If someone says, 'I love God,' and hates his brother, he is a liar; for he that does not love his brother who he can see, how can he love God whom he has not seen."

We can likewise see a progressive hardening in a historical context as we look at mankind in the scriptures. Man goes from nakedness, to covering themselves with leaves, to hiding in a bush, to eventually wearing armor. Armor is the ultimate natural indication of the hardness of the heart. It is worn with the intent of protecting the heart from others who intend to damage it. Again, this is a depiction with spiritual significance. Many of us know what it is to have a heart that is guarded by and buried under armor for fear of pain? However, we do not realize that the same armor protecting our hearts from mankind guards our hearts against interacting with God.

Here is an example. A person once sought me to pray for a potentially serious medical condition. So I prayed for them that the examination would go well. After the examination the person returned to me to share the results with me. After sharing the results the conversation took a strange turn. The person relayed to me that under the heavy mental stress of the situation that they had an emotional breakdown prior to arriving and during the examination. What made it strange to me was the fact that the person was mystified by the idea that they had an emotional breakdown. Now I remind you that this person was facing a very, very serious situation. Crying at any level was definitely appropriate.

The person asked me to help them understand the reason for the breakdown. I thought it was such a strange question but I knew how to answer it. I simply shared with them that the person crying was the one buried and hidden away. This person had experienced tremendously painful situations in their childhood all the way up through college. What they did to protect themselves from further pain was build up an amour made of confidence, self-reliance, and fight and they completely buried their perceived the weaker qualities underneath the armor. That means that everyone who encountered the person on the surface experienced opposition. The person on the surface was the façade. It was the person that was meant to be seen.

This person had buried within themself part of their real identity to survive. Consequently everything in life was approached as a fight and they always struggled to find intimacy with people. Then the person encountered God and began to relax. The process of becoming naked with God makes us let down our defenses. It makes us vulnerable! Not long after a real encounter with God we may find ourselves having to confront the person that we have hidden away.

This all points back to the reality that we all need some form of inner healing. Inner healing helps to soften our hearts so that we can hear God's voice clearly. If we look again at the demoniac you will see how Jesus resolved this man's pain. First, He brought awareness to the specific issues that were between Himself and this man. He said to the issue, "What is your name." For the first time this man knew why he was having a problematic life. Jesus put a face on this man's pain. Again, this is important. Some people think that it is a sin to feel pain. For this reason many people are bound to hidden pain in their heart. What they do not realize is that hidden pain still reveals itself in our life and relationships. In fact we can see this in the demonic as well. The Bible says that he lived in the tombs. This means that even though he was alive he preferred to keep company with those that were dead, even though he had access to the living. And even when he came around the living he would fight them to the point that they often bound him in chains. His pain was causing problems in his relationships.

Therefore, when Jesus encountered him He identified the issue and peeled back the layers of pain until what was reveled was the original heart. He removed the armor and under all of that pain was a man with a heart. God helped him to regain transparency. It was only at the point of purity from these influences that he was able to hear the voice of God speak into his life clearly. When he did, he got clear direction for his life. Jesus said, "Go and tell them what God has done for you" (Luke 8:39). In other words I'm bringing you into a place of destiny—Preach the gospel.

Moving forward you will come to see that hearing clearer is a process of softening the heart and making us comfortable to be transparent before God. God wants us to have a heart of flesh.(See Ezek. 36:26)

There is a very good reason to deal with pain accordingly. It is also visible in our story of the demoniac. You will further notice in the story that the man's pain has a voice. His issues spoke for him! Many people do not really consider the fact that pain, anger, bitterness, hatred, wrath, lust, fear, etc. all have a voice.

Just think back to an offense you have yet to resolve. Notice how the offense causes your inner voice to rant and rave. You may even notice a few ungodly choice words surfacing. This all happens because we have unresolved pain or a hardened heart.

Now, I want you to imagine, trying to hear God's voice with anger, rage, wrath, hatred, and company trying to speak. All of a sudden, there is a storm of noise inside you that drowns out the voice of God. Not only does it drown out the sound of God's voice, it also drives your focus from heavenly things to earthly things.

This is also what we see happening as we look back at the text with

Elijah. We see that the voice of pain has driven him into a place of self-awareness, and dimmed his God awareness.

Is this an invitation to push past pain? Again, absolutely not! Elijah did not push past his pain, but took that pain to God. God in the place of the sudden voice deals with Elijah's pain. Upon hearing God ask him what he was doing in that place, Elijah said, "I have been very zealous for the Lord God of hosts; because the children of Israel have forsaken your covenant, torn down your altars, and killed your prophets with the sword. I alone am left and they seek to take my life." My point in this section is that when we neglect to deal with our pain in the dark caves of life, we are susceptible to loosing our focus.

My Personal Experience

God called me to a ministry of revelation when I was very young. He also did so while I was a member of a Baptist Church that had little experience with the supernatural. Therefore my experiences with God were viewed as somewhat abnormal. Unlike most people who have encountered rejection regarding their prophetic gift, mine was embraced. Now some of you may be thinking, "What then was the problem?" The problem was that people began coming to me asking me what God was saying. A few of them referred to me as the man that God speaks to like Moses. And at first it did not bother me. In my mind I was fulfilling my calling.

On one occasion, a retreat, I was bombarded with questions. It was so bad that the leaders had to make the other participants leave me alone so that I could receive ministry. This was how it was and I didn't think much of it. That was until I started to feel as though no one really seemed that interested in me. The key words being "I began to feel..." This is important to the story. Many times I felt this way despite the invitations to hangout and enjoy life. But there were few occasions where I was not sought out for some type of counsel. After a while, I was overwhelmed and spiritually drained. Then I started to feel as though many of them were only interested in the gift. No one asked how I was doing or if I needed prayer or anything else. I was a prophetic counselor who needed human counsel and no one was there to meet the need—I felt a bit used.

Then as time passed I started hiding my gift. It was not long before the gift was in a dormant status. And I didn't even think about it. I still prayed and I still heard from God. I just did not freely speak to the people of God. After a while I became comfortable with hiding. I found that I could be around people and they were not asking me questions and probing my head. I had a normal Christian life and I was cool with that for a while. I was just like Adam and Eve hiding among the bushes. Have you ever wondered why they chose to hide in the bushes? To understand their choice you must consider that they were already covered with fig leaves. Adam and Eve chose to hide among the trees because it was easier to blend in. This is what I had done. I was blending in among those is the pews because it was easier than standing out in the pulpit.

As time went on however, the gift began calling me. It was just as Jeremiah described in his book. It was His word burning in my heart so that I was weary of holding it back. But now it was years later and the gifts came back stronger than ever. But I had developed an amour behind which I hid to prevent me from being used again and I found great comfort in that place.

So what was I to do? I wanted to please God and I longed for my ministry, but I also wanted to be viewed as normal. This was a problem. I did not realize the extent of the problem until I heard a Bishop Jakes sermon that challenged the audience stay connected to the body of Christ. What he taught us was based on Ephesians 4 which says that the growth of the body is caused by what each person supplies. That means that when we refuse to use our gifts we shortchange God's people and that's what I was doing in the local body.

You may be thinking what does he mean by the term "local" body. You see I had by this time started my online ministry. I did not at the time view myself as shortchanging the body. In my mind I was supplying the global body. But God challenged me that day about the local body. I had not served in that capacity within the local congregation in many years. I used my ministry gifts outside the church and served the church with my occupational gifts. I was hiding so that I could be normal and ensure that I did not get used again. It was pain hiding in my heart and I didn't even know it. That was until Bishop Jakes concluded.

At the conclusion he made an alter call for those who felt that the word spoke to their heart. All of a sudden I burst into tears as memories of being used came flooding into my mind. I had pain that I had forgotten to give to God and it was prohibiting me from pursuing the fullness of my ministry. I found myself crying out saying, "God they hurt me. They used me. They never cared anything about me as a person." I gave it all over to God that day so that I could let down my amour and come from behind the bushes. I was learning to be me again and Bishop Jakes words helped me accept my role in the body.

This encounter helped me to understand things that were happening in my life. Things such as why God's voice was clearer at various times. I observed that there were times when I felt comfortable I my own skin and with God's spiritual design for my life. In those times I also heard Him so incredibly clear. Then I noticed that when I was hiding and felt uncomfortable being me, that I struggled to hear clearly. After observing this for a while I began making the connection between the two experiences.

To help us make the connection Adam and Eve again help to make this clear. I want you to notice that God put them into the garden naked and it says that they were not ashamed. This was His design for them. Then they encountered a voice that caused them to experience shame and all of a sudden they were ashamed their nakedness which was God's design for their life. They were now less comfortable being who they were called to be. In their uncomfortable state they hid from God's presence. This means they were limiting their ability to commune with God.

Here is something interesting to note. When Adam and Eve fell into sin they were naked. They were in a state of transparency and vulnerability. When God was ready to resolve sin in world. He took Jesus to the cross naked. Again this means that He was transparent and vulnerable. In fact the last seven words of Christ were words of transparency. There is something about getting naked and living naked before God that opens our heart to hear clearly.

Here is something else to think about in regards to nakedness. Adam and Eve were the only unclothed thing in the garden. Jesus said God clothed the lilies of the field (See Matt.6:8). Animals had bodies clothed in fur. See creatures were clothed with the ocean and arrayed in scales. But man was naked. Why would God clothe everything but man? It was because mankind was the only thing God created for the purpose of communion. And true communion does not take place outside of transparency and vulnerability!

The Need for Inner Healing

For this reason we must also understand that pain requires inner healing. And more than likely, deliverance! I know that this is a "touchy" subject among many in the church, but it is one that should be seriously considered. While I call the demoniac man's issues "pain", I do realize that the pain is caused by demons—Demons that have a voice.

Nevertheless, whether you agree or disagree with Christians having demons, we can all agree that pain has a voice. For that reason, I courage you to research deliverance or inner healing and get your pain resolved so that you can hear God's voice clearly. You will find that it is absolutely crystal clear when there are no competing inner voices.

If you decide to explore the doctrines of demonology and deliverance, I recommend you start with Frank Hammond, *Pigs in the Parlor.*

The Power of Confession

One thing I tell people over and over again is that I am a big advocate of people seeing counselors and therapists. I know that this is another controversial view depending on the type of church you attend. Some people do not believe in counseling for Christians. In their mind the Lord is their counselor. I would however like to challenge each person reading this book to embrace the idea of counseling.

Why you say, should I embrace counseling? You should embrace counseling because James lays out a truth for us that leads to the healing you so desire. He says, **"...Confess your faults one to another that you may be healed."** Now to be fair, James is referring to natural healing. Or is he! I would go into further detail on what I mean by the latter statement but that is a subject best covered in another book. Nonetheless, the principle of the passage is that sometimes things that require healing must first be exposed. I don't think that this truth applies only to natural healing. I believe it also applies to spiritual healing.

Sometimes to get healed from inner pain we need to lie on someone's couch and tell them about the secrets hidden in our past. Just ask those who have experienced a traumatic childhood how tormented they are by the pain of those memories. Many times people go throughout life carrying dark secrets that they try to resolve with alcohol, sex, drugs, and other things. Likewise, more often than not these people are identified by their visible struggle. They are kin to the Gadarene demoniac. The people saw the anger, rage, and pain. But Jesus saw the man hiding underneath! And that's what a good counselor does. They help people to look past their façade and the unhealthy choices of life to see the precious person on the inside. And one of the ways they do this is by using the model Jesus set. They put a face on the cause of the pain, help to peel it back, and establish value in the person. Notice that in Jesus' counseling session the result is called a healing even though there was nothing physically wrong! Do you need inner healing? Is it a good idea to get counseling? These are just some ideas to consider for those who want to get out of the bushes and get back to being naked. Again I remind you that it was God's intention and design for Adam and Eve to be naked!

This is my final thought on this issue that I would like you to consider. Jesus spent a lot of time speaking to the demoniac's pain. The majority of the story is Jesus communicating with the man through his pain. But when the pain was removed and the man was healthy, Jesus' voice was loud and clear in his life. The same happened to Elijah. God spoke to him in the dark place of his life. But what was unclear in the cave was clear in the light. God never answered Elijah's pain in the cave. But in 1 Kings 19:15-16 God provided a remedy for his pain!

Elijah's change was waiting for him at the entrance. The entrance represents the place of opportunity. Are you missing an opportunity because pain has you sleeping in the dark places in your life?

Get up and get to the opportunity that God has waiting for you. The answer you seek is not in the cave. It's at the door—it is not in the dark but in the light!

10 | It's a Process

Hopefully it is evident that God spoke to Elijah in a voice. Again, I understand that this is going to be hard for many people to embrace. However, you should know that learning to use your spiritual ears to hear is a process. I said to God as He spoke to me about this issue, "Lord, how do we get there?" I asked Him this question because I was not hearing this way consistently. This was His response to me, "Elijah had to get up, and take the necessary steps towards the entrance." In other words, it's a process. Again Hebrews says our senses must be exercised by reason of use. You will find this to be true with all of the spiritual senses.

One thing that we must come to acknowledge is the reality that all things in life are a part of a process. New lives come into the earth by the process of creation. Food goes through a process before it arrives on our plate. Likewise a tree starts as a seed and grows into something more. It is all comes down to process.

We can look through the scriptures and see that God is also a God of process. Just look at Abraham for example. God spoke to him years earlier to plant an idea in his heart. It was a dream that we can see go through a process before it is fulfilled. The idea of process is most notable in the life of Joseph. God told Joseph that he would be a lord over his entire family. Then he was put into a pit, then sold into slavery, then put into prison. Finally he landed in the palace as the second in command to the leader of the free world! Joseph arrived at God's destination, but not outside of God's process.

God told Joseph that he would make him a leader. Then God put him in places where he was able to exercise his leadership ability. First he was a leader among the slaves. Then he was the leader in the prison. This was all a part of God's training process to make Joseph a leader capable of handling the position in the palace.

This may seem a bit trivial to some reading. Our advancing technological generation has done everything possible to eliminate process from our lives. But whether a machine does the processing or a human, nothing escapes the idea of process.

The interesting thing about process is the fact that it conveys to us that to each part of the process, there is a time associated with development. This is a truth that also applies to hearing the voice of God. I wish that I could tell you to do steps 1, 2, 3, 4, and 5, to produce the desired result. That however would not be the truth. The reality is that developing good spiritual hearing takes time and commitment. Consequently, so does developing any of the spiritual senses.

I once debated a person on social media who made the comment, "A person cannot be taught the voice of God!" I told him that his assessment was not properly founded. I then went on to explain to him that the Bible is clear in presenting us with the idea that prophets were apart of schools. 1 Kings show us this when Elisha followed Elijah around from city to city (See 2 Kings 2:1-10). The fact that there were schools meant that there were those in that place that taught and those that were learning.

The fact that there were those learning in a school environment for prophets provides us with even more information. A prophet is one that "hears" and "speaks" from God what he has heard or seen. In the context of our discussion, this means that prophets in training were learning how to "hear" as well as how to speak. This also means that there was a time of development—a process.

You should consider that if the prophets in the Old Testament had to go through a process to learn how to hear God's voice. You will have to go through a process of learning as well. This also means learning how to fail.

Remember, our goal is to move from a faint whisper to a clearly discernable voice. During this process there will be days when the voice of God is absolutely loud and clear. Likewise, there will be days of hearing a faint whisper. The key to growing through this process is learning what is creating this gap in performance. This is where you need to consider the four reasons for which you may be hearing a still small voice. I have learned to use this list of reasons God provided me to weed out any hearing problems and take appropriate action.

The Art of Listening

This is also, why it is so important that we to learn how to practice listening. The practice of listening is a part of the process of better hearing. Getting better at hearing clearer is all about developing a habit of tuning in and listening. Before this book ends I am going to provide you with some activities that you can do to practice listening to God.

There is one thing to which I can testify, that is the reality that hearing clearly involves work. Remember, one of the key reasons people do not hear clearly is a lack of focus. There are times when God starts talking and I am focused. That is until something distracts me and I find my mind wandering into the days activities. Then it wanders back to God and He starts talking again. This is what I call the "see saw hearing" affect. This simply means that we must work harder to develop a habit of listening.

This idea of developing a habit of listening came directly from God. One day He spoke to me early in the morning as I was getting dressed. He said, "Face to face. Don't aim low". He was encouraging me to not stop at seeing dreams and visions. He wanted me to aim for "face-to-face" communion like Moses. He then reminded me that He placed a higher value on face-to-face communion than dreams and visions (See Numbers 12:6). As He continued talking I became distracted with the process of getting ready for work. The minute my focus shifted so did my hearing.

This problem may seem unique to our communion with God, but I assure you that it is not. As humans we often struggle in our face-to-face communion with each other. If you are honest, you realize that it is near impossible to stay engaged in a conversation and a television program at the same time. The pull of the two for your attention ultimately starts an internal war. All of a sudden you are is a battle for what is most important and most interesting. For this reason we have many books on active listening. By far it is generally agreed upon by all that listening is a skill that develops with practice—practice that involves a process.

Therefore, as you endeavor to learn and grow in going from a still small voice to the clear voice of God, give yourself permission to grow. It is a process of learning and growing closer in your walk with God. Let the learning experience be a pleasant one and not one of frustration.

11 | Gaining Clarity

Another thing I want to write about is the benefit of hearing the voice of God. In our study of Elijah's experience we saw something interesting. When the word of the Lord came to him in the cave the author was able to articulate what God said. When Elijah heard the voice at the entrance of the cave the author was again able to articulate what was said. However, when the author wrote about the still small voice, there was no clarity as to what was said. This happens more than enough times with a lot of people having a sense of uncertainty as it pertains to the voice of God.

One reason God wants to encourage us to push into the voice of God is so that we will not be so overwhelmed with uncertainty. The still small voice often times leaves people in the place of saying to themselves, "I think God is saying something to me". God wants us to know that we can hear clearly what He is saying. Again Jesus said, "My sheep hear my voice and I call them by name" (See John 10:3). That means we can expect to hear clearly.

Just consider what Jesus is really saying in the passage. He says "He calls them individually **by name!**" In other words each one of us can hear God as clear as Samuel when God called his name. This means that

God's voice in the believer's life is not a corporate sound that envelopes an atmosphere in which we pull something down. But to the contrary, His voice is heard by each of us as a distinct sound that we can identify. It is a sign of clarity!

So many times I have seen articles, online posts, and books that recommend getting to a quiet place to hear God's voice. It is usually recommended that you do so in the morning so that you can quiet your soul. The idea presented in these writings and teachings is that God can be heard whispering in the quiet.

For this reason I am adamant about us coming into a place of being able to hear the clear voice of God. First, let me start by saying that I absolutely agree with the aforementioned principles. You do need to learn how to still your soul. However, this should be the starting point. You should not be limited by "the quiet of morning" in your availability to God. To really be used by God you should be available to hear from Him at anytime.

I give the same advice to those who live on dreams. The entirety of your Christian service cannot be spent on the mattress. You must come to a place where you are available to God during the waking hours.

Let's take Philip the evangelist for example. In Acts 8:29, we read about him walking down the road when God suddenly spoke to him to minister to a stranger sitting in a chariot. That sudden moment of availability changed a man's life. In fact I would dare say that it impacted an entire nation. Just imagine what opportunity might have been lost if Philip was limited to dreaming or to the quiet of the morning. In order for him to be valuable in that particular situation, he needed to be available to hear from God. And to hear suddenly and clearly in that moment!

His effectiveness was directly related to his availability. His willingness to be open to hear God's voice exposed the Ethiopians to the Gospel.

The Benefits of Clarity

So what are the benefits of clarity in regard to hearing God's voice? There are two benefits in particular that I would like to discuss. 1) Having a sense of certainty and 2) Getting precise instructions.

Having clarity means knowing exactly what to do. It is not guessing, or feeling like the Lord is saying something. It is not believing what the Lord is saying, but clearly knowing His will for your life at any given moment.

One thing that surprises me is the gap between the early church and the current dispensation of the church. In the early church people engaged God in visions and dreams, worked as partners with angels, heard the voice of the Spirit of God and obeyed, and even heard very specific information from God. But in our dispensation pastors get up to preach and don't know if it was God that gave them their sermon. We also see prophets that know what God is saying to others but whose lives reek of those who can't discern His voice for their personal life. We also see people who can't move on what they hear in prayer until someone confirms that what they heard came from God. We do not see any such examples in the scriptures. Now this does not mean that it is not a good practice. After all the Bible says let every word be established in the mouth of two or three witnesses (Deut. 18:16). It also says, "In the multitude of counselors there is safety"(Prov. 15:22). But you will not find any examples in the scriptures of people that lingered in uncertainty until these two principles were fulfilled in their life!

For instance in Acts 9:10-19, we see a man named Ananias, whom the Bible refers to as just a disciple. While in prayer he had a vision of Jesus. In the vision Jesus gave him precise information regarding the address of a man, the city, the street, and the name of the person he was to visit. Not only does he see in detail but he also dialogs with Jesus in the experience! I want you to know that it was all he needed. He did not have to pray about it. He did not get a second opinion about it. He just got up with absolute certainty and obey God's voice. Hearing the clear voice of God created in him a level of certain knowing and allowed him to receive precise instructions.

We likewise see the same thing in Peter's life. Peter fell into a trance and heard a clear voice. I know you are saying but he was in a vision. But after the vision ended he again heard the clear voice of God. Acts 10:19-20 says, that as he pondered the meaning of the vision that the Spirit spoke to him and said, there are three men at the door to see you. I sent them go with them doubting nothing (paraphrased).

Again I want to note that he did not have to confer with the counsel of the other apostles or get a confirmation. He knew with certainty that it was God that spoke to him, no questions asked. Likewise he knew "exactly" what God wanted him to do. He had precise instruction that allowed him to operate confidently in the plan of God for his life at that moment.

We can look to Elijah as further confirmation of this truth. When we look at 1 Kings19 there are some important pieces of information to discern to really understand what was happening in that chapter. First we need to know that Elijah did not choose to hide from Jezebel on a randomly chosen mountain. Mount Horeb was a historic place for Israel. It was the place where Moses met God at the burning bush and it was the place where the 10 commandments were given. It was a symbolic place of direction and instruction. Elijah had gone to the mountain known to be frequented by God to hear from Him.

His idea paid off. This much we know because God's voice is heard three distinct times in the passage. Two of those instances involved clear communication from God. One, the still small voice, was unclear. But of these three occurrences only one of them provided the prophet with the clearest of instructions. The one instance that provided clear and precise instructions was the "sudden voice". Again we see that precise and certain instructions are heard in hearing the clear voice of God.

So as you endeavor to learn about God and His ways, know that you can get precise direction from God. I would like to close out this chapter with a challenge. I want you to look at all the scriptures regarding the voice of God and see how many times God spoke in a way that left the recipient unsure of His expectations. I am certain that you will not find one! God always spoke with clear and precise direction and He will do it for you too!

12 | Tuning Into the Right Frequency

I once had the pleasure of ministering to a guy on social media who suffered from hearing voices. At the time he was terribly tormented and had come off of his medication. When I met him he was asking me whether or not he should continue with his medications. He was a fairly new Christian and had heard that medication opened doors for demons. For this reason he stopped taking his medication. As I pondered what he was asking me I heard God say clearly, "Tell him to take the medication." As I still sat pondering the situation God repeated himself. From there I began an email dialogue with this guy about his condition.

I told him that he was not imagining the voices. I told him that they were real. Part of the torment he endured was having a very real experience that did not line up with reality. I dare to say that most people with these types of mental disorders are really gifted in spiritual hearing. Some of you may disagree. But if his problem were sensing things he didn't see we would acknowledge it as a gift. We would say he was a gifted feeler or some type of physic. But when this happens in our hearing gifts we are not as welcoming to this idea.

I have learned that in our western culture we are more welcoming of those who dream than we are of those that hear voices. Just think about it. If you were to say to a group of friends that you had a dream, a lively discussion would begin. In fact your friends would likely share their own dreams with the group. But if you said you heard a voice, the room would become eerily silent. Yet the Bible is full of men and women who heard a voice. And they recorded what the voice said and it was canonized and named the Bible. I bet you have never thought about it that way. We live our lives by the recorded words of people who heard voices. They heard God's voice and they heard the voice of angels. So while it may not be welcoming in theory to hear a voice, the reality is that every Christian makes hard life decisions based on the things they read in the Bible—which was given by a voice. That's just something to think about!

This young man was hearing voices and people told him that they were not real. But they were. I later discovered that not only could he hear spiritually, but he could see spiritually as well. He just needed to know what was happening to him. So I began to share with him and encourage him in how to hear correctly. He also watched my YouTube series to learn how to discern God's voice.

There are a lot to things that we regularly experience that are spiritual in nature. Many of these things we ignore or lightly regard. For instance, I am a natural daydreamer. In fact I was such a daydreamer growing up that it interfered with my schoolwork. However, during my daydreams I would have what is referred to as déjà vu. As I grew up I became less sensitive to what I was seeing because I was taught to resist it. Then God taught me what was happening and to write down what I see when I'm daydreaming. Looking for the daydreams have made me more sensitive to them when they occur.

The spiritual abilities of seeing and feeling are the same way. In fact as I was writing this essay I had a déjà vu recall. I remembered that I would be working on a paper for someone I met online, and that my boss would come out of his office and interrupt me. The moment I realize it I said, my boss is going to come out of the office. Then I stopped writing and waited. Two minutes later he come out of the office to my desk. So there are a lot of things that we bypass that are spiritual abilities and I was trying to help this guy to hone his.

As I continued to share with him I said to him, "You must be tuning in to hear the voices. The only way to hear the voices is that you are giving them your attention." To which he replied with shock, "Yeah, I told my doctors it's like tuning into a radio." I knew that he had a hearing gift that was being manipulated by demonic forces. They were operating on the principle of "focus". They would curse and say vulgar things to get his attention. Then when he turned aside to listen to what they had to say the show would really begin.

Later he listened to my YouTube series on spiritual warfare and learned how to deal with what was happening in his life. Then he emailed me a few months later and reported that he had almost gained complete sanity.

So what is the point of this story? The point is, one, these principles are spiritual principles. They apply across the board to spiritual communication. In fact in Job 4:12-18 Job's friend had a dream in which a spirit engaged him in communication. It says, "In disquieting thoughts from the visions of the night". This shows us that when all is quiet on the inside then the voice of any spiritual being can be heard—good or evil. They all operate from the same principles. And hearing is as simple as tuning into the right frequency.

Years ago when I first started hearing God's voice clearly, I also realized that I could hear the voices of demons as well. Initially they harassed me in much the same manner they harassed this guy. They would curse to get my attention. Then in my pride, I would argue with them. That was until God said to me one day as they were attempting to get my attention, "Don't speak to them. They are trying to make you familiar with their voice." That experience stuck in my mind and I began to understand the term "familiar spirit".

This means that we must be discerning about what and who we listen to. I do not advocate becoming obsessive about the matter, but it should be considered.

A lot of material written on the subject of voice of God casually mentions the idea of discernment. It is usually a chapter in length with vague principles for discernment. I believe that discernment should account for a large portion of content in a book on this subject. Some people would like to believe that God would not allow us to be deceived. That is a truth that I wholeheartedly agree with. The problem with this idea however, is that we forget that we are creatures of free will. As such, you are perfectly capable of opening the door to deception for yourself.

If we can open the door to deception, then what is God's responsibility in protecting us? God's responsibility is not to make decisions for you, but to provide us with what us need to make our own decisions. For this reason He gave us a Bible to study. If we live within the confines He provides we will be safe.

He has also provided us with the gift of discerning of spirits. This gift is exclusively responsible for helping us in distinguishing what is of God and what is not. Some people like to use the passage, "If you ask for a fish God will not give you a rock" as their safety net (See Matt. 7:9). Then they willingly launch out into things that they really know nothing about.

The problem is that God is not the only "giver". Satan gives as well. In Luke 4:6 Satan said to Jesus, I will "give" you the whole world if you will bow down and worship me. For it is under my control and I "give" it to whomever I wish. This means that it is possible to be deceived. Just consider the many unfulfilled prophetic utterances that came from dreams and visions. Those supernatural experiences were rooted in a spiritual source!

So learning to discern and tuning into the right frequency is important. I also tell people that it not about the rock or the fish that God gives you. It about whether you know the difference between the two!

13 | The Voice I Know or the Voice I Hear

If it is possible that we can tune in to hear the voice of God, what markers provide safety for us in the experience? One comes from Jesus. He said My sheep hear "My" voice. The key words being, "My sheep", "My voice", and "hear". The word "hear" in the Greek means to perceive and to heed. What Jesus is saying is that my sheep will only tune in or give their attention to My voice. He is likewise clear to say why. He says a stranger's voice they will not follow for they do not know the voice of strangers. The word "know" means to know by experience. Notice that he does not say that they do not hear the stranger's voice, but that the voice of the stranger is foreign to them. Jesus' voice creates a confident knowing that commands our attention.

I like to use this illustration to make this point. When you go out to dinner with someone to a crowed restaurant, there are always multiple conversations going on around you. With all of these conversations happening around you, you can only hear the conversation that you give your attention to. Likewise when it comes to hearing God's voice over the other voices competing for your attention, you need not worry. God's voice has qualities to it that cause us to hear his voice clearly above the rest.

In my book *God, Is that You, Me, or the Devil*, I go into great detail contrasting the ways God speaks, what He talks about, verses how the enemy speaks. It is a very extensive document on the subject. Therefore, what I am attempting to address in the paragraphs to follow is only a fraction of a subject that needs real consideration.

The Front Door or the Back Door

Not only does Jesus tell us that we hear His voice, He also lays out a stark contrast between Himself and the stranger. He says in (John 10:1). The stranger is a thief who does not enter by the door. He's sneaky. Jesus however is clear that He stands at the door and calls His sheep. My point is this. The enemy will always sneak in because the goal is to be unnoticed.

You can see this aspect of his character in the Garden of Eden. He appeared as a serpent in the garden for a reason. He needed to sneak into a conversation with Eve. So he used a creature she felt comfortable speaking to. He was not a stranger to her family. Her husband was the one responsible for giving it a name. She had encountered the serpent before! He was being sneaky and trying to be undetected.

God however is very direct. Jesus said he comes to the front door. Likewise, we can see this aspect of God everywhere in the scripture. Jesus clearly announces himself and says, "I am the way, the truth and the life…"(See John 14:6). Have you ever considered the fact that the only spiritual being that does not promote an awareness of his existence is Satan? Think about it for a second. Satan is disguised as false prophets of many religions. He also displays himself through various false religions, but he is never open about it. In fact he has worked really hard to convince the world that he is a myth and a fairytale. He never announces himself. He operates this way so that he can move against you as stealth.

Not so with God. He has been out front and self-proclaiming of His greatness since the book of Genesis. The Bible says lift up your gates you everlasting doors and the King of Glory shall come in (Psa. 27:7). God will always use the door. He says I stand at "the door" and knock… He never sneaks in some other way. (See Rev. 3:20) That will always be the thief!

For instance in Job 4:12-17 one of Job's friends has a dream and in the dream he describes a spirit that he encounters. He said "…and I was not able to discern its form." In other words, I was not sure who or what it was speaking to me. Common sense should have told him that God historically in the scriptures appears in a clear discernable form. No one ever saw God and didn't know that it was Him. He said to me as He spoke to me about this subject, "My sheep know My voice. If you don't know then you don't know". He was saying if you are unclear then it's not me. My voice is clear and you know Me when I speak.

One Gathers, the Other Scatters

There is another contrast to see in John 10. Jesus says His voice gathers, but the enemy will cause the sheep to scatter. What does this mean? God's voice is not distracting. He causes us to have focus in our life. Satan's voice on the other hand causes us to scatter. This idea of the enemy scattering the sheep has three connotations. One, his voice creates confusion. Two, it creates division. And three, it exalts us above the fold.

1) **Confusion.** Satan's voice will always create confusion. In fact the Bible says that where confusion and self- seeking are present there will also be every evil thing (James 3:16). Be careful in general of voices (spiritual or natural) that cause confusion. Confusion leads to scattering. That also includes confusion of the mind. Sometimes we can see confusion within groups and it is easy to identify that it is Satan. But sometimes we get mental confusion caused by an idea that Satan plants in our mind.

I want to remind you that Satan wants you to trade God's idea for his idea. He will always be the voice that creates confusion in your mind.

2) **Division.** Jesus said that a house divided against itself cannot stand (Mark 3:25). We should note that Jesus is acknowledging that Satan's house is not divided. He is also cluing us in to the reality that Satan is aware that division is a key component in overcoming a strongman. Therefore, you should know that God does not create division. In fact Paul mentions several times that we are to be of one mind, one accord, and one spirit. (See Phil. 2:2, 1 Pet. 3:8, Rom. 15:16)

3) **Exaltation.** The last thing I want to point out is that the enemy's voice is one of pride. I can always tell when someone is listening to the wrong voice when the voice they hear seeks to set them apart (above) the flock. I know that soon after they are going to somehow experience a fall. I usually try to bring them down to earth with Amos 3:7. This verse simply says that "God will do nothing unless He reveals His secret to His servants (plural) the prophets (plural)". Unique revelation is usually a sign of error. This voice usually takes the form of a person hearing how renown they will be. People such as Jim Jones and David Karesh are classic examples of wayward Christians that exalt themselves above the rest of the body of Christ. They are not alone however; today there are many voices in our churches that do the same.

Such persons usually use their self-exalted position to cause their flocks to separate themselves from others, i.e. other believers, family members, friends, etc. Under their state of delusion, their followers are told that all other churches are wrong. All those who operate under this type of abusive spirit hear voices that encourage scattering.

Before I close out my thoughts on this particular section regarding scattering, I need to address an issue. That issue is the difference between separation and exaltation. There is no doubt in my mind that someone will argue that the word "holy" means to be separated. This will most certainly be "pride" talking.

The word "holy" means to set apart or to set aside. Exaltation means "to set up or over". Hopefully, the difference is obvious. God's voice may set us apart or to the side of others. He may do so for a special purpose. In contrast, pride seeks to set us over others. People responding to pride don't seek to move over. They seek to move up!

Jesus is our example. He would often separate Himself for prayer. Then He would come back and serve. He went aside and down. Not aside and up and over. God's voice led to humility in His life and ministry, not pride and arrogance.

In this time of doomsday prophets, we really need to know this truth. So many people are being scattered by voices of judgment. I am not implying that God does not give us words or judgment. However, I am trying to communicate that His voice gathers us in trying times, not scatters us with fear.

Here is an example from my life of Satan at work to scatter. What I am going to share with you will be a revelation to some. It may even be familiar to a few. Yet for some others it will be challenge to consider.

In my many years as a Christian I have come to realize that some people have not embraced the understanding that we must be discerning. If you really consider all of Hebrews 6:14 we see that the exercising of our senses is for the purpose of learning to discern between good and evil. It implies that good is not obvious and neither is evil. The idea presented is one of distinguishing counterfeits. What is most important about what the writer of Hebrews is telling us is that good may appear as evil and vice versa. Therefore, we must acknowledge that not all of our dreams and spiritual communication is from God. What I am going to share is a dream that was demonic in nature. As I share it I will tell what it was meant to accomplish and how it relates to the principle of scattering.

One night as I attempted to fall asleep I heard a vulgar statement regarding my wife. Of course this was not the voice of God! It was a demon that I more than likely picked up in a healing encounter. Earlier in the day I taught a young man how to take control over sickness in his body so that he could speak healing to himself. As he followed my instructions he was getting relief from the spirit that brought the sickness. These kinds of encounters always invite some form of retaliation.

That being the case, as I lay down and closed my eyes I had a dream. In the dream my wife and I were preparing for an intimate moment and we were trying to do so before the kids awakened. As the dream continued my wife started folding clothes. At which time I became angry and said to her, "There you go. You are putting me second again!" As the dream progressed and I became angry I began to develop an awareness of the fact that I was dreaming. As I did, I realized that this was a lie. I did not feel this way, nor did my wife and I have these types of problems. Realizing that a demon was using a dream to sow a seed I promptly rebuked it and discarded the idea from my mind.

As we examine the dream we have to realize that every seed watered produces fruit. Understanding this principle allowed me to realize the potential fruit of the idea. The fruit of the dream's idea was to cause confusion in my marriage by putting a lie in my mind. It was also intended to obviously create division. Last, it was devised with the idea of exalting my selfish needs above that of my wife's. She needed to do her chores, I needed to be intimate. My need was no more important than hers. All of this is a clear depiction of the principle of "scattering".

Selfless vs. Selfish

Another contrast that is also found in Jesus' declaration is found in the statement that says He gives his life for the sheep. This is not the character of Satan. In fact it says the hireling flees for he does not care for the sheep. God's voice is giving and Satan's voice is selfish. Likewise, his voice makes you self-centered.

When you hear the voice of God, ask yourself if it is pointing back to you. This again goes back to self-exaltation and self-centeredness. I can remember two instances in particular that are relevant to this idea.

In the first instance, I remember a time when I would have fanciful visions at church during worship. They were visions of me standing on stage laying hands on the sick. Seems innocent doesn't it. However, that was not all that I saw in these visions. The clue for me that this was not a vision from God was realized in the moment that I saw how impressed everyone was with me. The visions seemed to be more about me than about God or the fact that people were healed.

I wish I could tell you that this has only happened to me. But I have been around the church for a long time. That being the case, I have seen others have these same types of visions—visions that usually prove to be fruitless. In my experience the only fruit that usually results from this type of voice is "pride" and "arrogance".

In my second encounter with this type of voice, I was hearing that my friend and I were the two great witnesses from the book of Revelations. Now keep in mind, at the time I was an evangelical having charismatic experiences. I thought I was unique and the devil tried to capitalize on my ignorance. This, however, was too far fetch for me to embrace. In this instance he was easy to discern.

All of this is in stark contrast to the nature of Jesus Christ. The Bible says "Esteem others better than yourself" (Phil. 2:3). It also says that Jesus, though He was God made himself a servant (See Phil. 2:6). This is a very different attitude than that of the one that leaves the sheep. In fact Jesus said of Himself, that He gives His life for the sheep (See John 10:11). The voice of God inspires us to give of ourselves not exalt ourselves.

A Call to Freedom or a Call to Bondage

The last contrast that the Holy Spirit points out in the passage is freedom vs. bondage. Jesus says that He calls His sheep by name and "leads them out". This tells us that God's voice is an agent of change. His leading the sheep is an indication that His voice, one, brings them out of bondage and two, provides them with direction. So whenever God speaks to us His voice makes us free. For the scriptures say, "You shall know the truth and the truth shall make you free" (See John 8:32). It also says, that the Holy Spirit is the spirit of truth (See John 16:13). God's voice makes us free!

The Holy Spirit also points out that the enemy's interest is in keeping the sheep in bondage. Notice, that he does not call to the sheep or lead them out, but he does allow them to be harassed. He sneaks in and creates problems. Any voice that you hear that holds you back from fulfilling God's instructions to you is the enemy's voice. And that includes any voice that encourages you to live in bondage to sin. Forgiveness and grace free us to pursue God and all that He has for us. It does not free us to live any way that we choose. So if you hear a voice that puts freedom in the hands of your oppressors it is not God's voice!

Here's an example. One of my faithful YouTube followers contacted me via post with a concern. She had a desire to start doing personal street level ministry. As she considered this possibility a loved one, whom she trusted, came to her and said, "God said women can't be ministers". This was the enemy attempting to keep her in the sheep pin. He wanted to hinder her forward movement into the things of God.

When she contacted me in regards to this situation. I gently took her through the scriptures and showed her all of the places where God himself made women leaders. This is an example of God's truth opening the door of the sheep pin and allowing us the freedom to follow Him.

We can see this truth all throughout the scriptures. Just looking back to Israel's freedom from slavery we can see this clearly. For it was God's word to them, "Let My people go", that brought them out of slavery. Likewise, we see Satan at work in the life of the Pharaoh trying to keep them in bondage. In fact they could only follow God if Pharaoh gave them the word to go. This story was about God's call to freedom and Satan's call to bondage. It was a battle of who had the mightiest word!

So remember, God's voice frees us to move forward and follow Him. Satan's voice keeps us in bondage. So ask yourself the question, do I feel free or oppressed after hearing a voice!

All of these principles are designed to give basic guidance regarding how to distinguish whose voice you are listening to.

14 | Getting Those Ears Open

I know what you're thinking. How can we go from the place of a still small voice to the voice of God? Some of it is easy when we consider the four reasons that may be the source of our hindrance to hearing clearly. One, if your problem is disobedience, then repent and obey His last command to you. That's the easy one. Spiritual warfare requires us to resist the devil. Resisting the devil can mean doing some house cleaning. Sometimes we need deliverance from demonic influence that pollutes our eyes and ears. If we learn submission to the will of God He gives us the power to resist the devil and then he will flee from us (See James 4:7). Likewise, pain requires spiritual healing and it is definitely a process. You may need to see a counselor or therapist. Last, a lack of focus means learning how to pay attention when God is speaking.

I saved "lack of focus" for last because it really is the starting point for getting into the deeper places. It is needed to develop sharper vision, feeling, and hearing. So how do we get there?

Perception

The starting point for hearing God's voice is "perception". The Bible says in Job 33:14, God may speak this way or that way but man does not perceive it, so God speaks to him at night in dreams. Notice that God is clearly trying to speak to man when he is awake but He says that man is not sensitive enough to recognize Him speaking. Elijah experiences the same thing with the still small voice. God said to me one day, "Kevin, the still small voice is the starting point, not the end goal". What God has taught me is that we must to pay attention to the things He uses to get our attention.

For instance, it was a whisper that got Elijah's attention. It was the burning bush that got Moses' attention. Elisha felt the hand of the Lord come upon him before he prophesied. Daniel saw in a dream images that made him keep looking. Jeremiah was in a potter's house watching a potter working with clay when he became aware of God's voice. Last, there was Philip the evangelist. He saw an Ethiopian Eunuch sitting in a chariot reading the scriptures. That's how God got his attention.

In all of these examples we can see that God uses various ways to get our attention, but we must be sensitive enough to perceive that it is God at work. Once we perceive that God is trying to get our attention, we must look deeper or listen more intently.

For me this happens in various ways. Sometimes I feel a heat coming upon me, or the presence of God fills the room. Sometimes I see shifts in the atmosphere. Sometimes it's a random picture or mental movie. I may also experience a sudden awareness or fascination with something in the natural that comes alive with meaning. However He does it, we must learn to be receptive to the idea that He is about to speak to us.

This goes back to the idea of "front door vs back door". God always allows us to be aware that He is speaking. One reason He operates this way is because He does not share His glory. Therefore, He makes us aware of His voice. Again this is in contrast to the voice of the enemy. He comes in through a way other than the front door. This is why we have discerning of spirits. This spiritual ability helps us to detect the presence of sneaky Satan. He is rarely open about the reality that he is communicating with you or that his motives are nefarious.

Tuning In

Colossians 3:2 teaches us a process and reveals the importance of our mind in the process. It says, "Set your mind on things above, not things of the earth". As we discussed in an earlier chapter, this has everything to do with focus. One thing this passage does is tells us, that we must make a decision with our will. It also tells us that we can use our will to direct our attention to earthly things or spiritual things.

Most people do not consider the reality that the scriptures connect our spirit to our minds. Most people have been taught that the successful spiritual life divorces the two. This point of view is completely opposite of what the scriptures actually teaches. This error in thinking is promoted by a popular teaching which is drawn from an incorrect interpretation of the scriptures.

The teaching states that the mind is an enemy of the spirit. This error in interpretation comes from Romans 8:7, which states that the carnal mind is enmity with God... However if you carefully read the entire section of text above and beneath this one passage, you will find that the mind must be transformed. If in fact the entire passage tells us that we must be "spiritually minded". A spiritual mind is a mind that is tuned to spiritual things. It is a condition of the mind—One that is set on things above.

When we look at the passage in Colossians one thing eludes our understanding. That one thing is seen in the statement "things above". This simple phrase tells us that God encourages us to think about spiritual things. We know this to be fact because the passage presents us with a comparison. Things above where Christ is seated speak of the invisible world. Things of the earth clearly speak of the visible world.

As it relates to the subject of the voice of God, this passage communicates to us that our focus must be on God. It is also a subtle indication that we use our minds to "tune in" to God's kingdom.

For me, God generally leads me into His presence with a song. The song I hear and how close or distant it sounds is everything. If it is distant or faint I know that my focus is off and that I am tuned to things of the earth. If I hear a loud distinct sound, I know that I am tuned into heaven. The interesting thing I've noticed is that when I am completely immersed in the things of the earth I cannot hear any music at all.

I am certain that someone is saying to himself or herself, show me some kind of scripture reference on this. Ephesians 5:19 says, "Be filled with the spirit, singing to yourselves in song, hymns, and spiritual song, singing and **making melody in your heart** to the Lord". Notice that singing and making melody in the heart is an indication of being filled with the Spirit. So what might we experience when we are not filled?

We don't realize it but the scriptures connect being filled by the Spirit with God speaking. We first see it in Ezekiel 2:1-2, it says that when the prophet encountered God something happened. It says, "As He spoke to me the Spirit entered me and set me on my feet; and I heard Him speaking to me…" It says it again in Ezekiel 3:24, " The Spirit entered me and made me stand on my feet, and He spoke with me…" Both of these passages show us that the prophet heard God speaking when he was "filled". We can also see this connection in Acts. Several times they were filled and spoke. What we see demonstrated in Acts is a fulfillment of what Jesus said to the disciples in Matthew 10:20. He also said to them, "Take no thought for what you will say, for it will be given to you in that hour, for it will be the Spirit of your father in you speaking". In other words, the Holy Spirit will speak to you by filling your mouth with what is to be said in the moment. So there is a connection between being filled and Gods voice.

In our section on perception I encouraged you to be sensitive to moments when God is trying to get your attention. A part of being sensitive means paying attention to the song in your heart. I promise you when God fills your heart with a song, He is filling you. He is also guiding your mind into focus. He uses this process to get us into His presence.

The Bible says, "Come before His presence with singing, enter His courts with praise" (See Ps. 95:2, 100:2). This tells us how God expects us to approach His throne. Likewise, it is the Spirit of God's job to teach us all things. All things include teaching us how to enter into the awareness of God's presence.

This means we must learn to be sensitive to God filling our heart with songs. Allow those songs to guide your mind into the presence (awareness) of God. You may even find yourself getting lost in the reality of God's presence. Not only will you become move acutely aware of His presence, but you will also notice clarity in God's voice.

15 | The Role of Faith in Hearing

This has been an interesting journey with the Holy Spirit. He has been challenging me over and over to share with His people that they can hear the clear voice of God. Initially, I thought to myself, these people are going to think I am crazy. Then one day after a long day at work and an even longer commute home, God filled me. I have learned over time that when God fills me, He's going to speak soon after. Therefore, I tuned in to hear what He wanted to say. It started as a desire to teach on the audible voice of God. Recognizing that this was the direction of God's leading, I listened more intently for what was sure to follow. This is what I heard. God said to me, "They hear a still small voice, because that is what they have been taught. I want you to teach them that they can hear My voice clearly. It will open up their faith to receive."

I thought that was an interesting thing to say. So often we are deficient in our understanding of how essential faith is to our Christian community. Hebrews 11:6 tells us that without faith we are not pleasing to God. Even our ability to receive the gospel is predicated on our ability to appropriate our faith. For it says, by "…grace you have been saved **through faith**…" (Eph. 2:8).

We can also see faith as it relates to hearing the voice of God. Romans

10:17 reads, "Faith comes by hearing and hearing by the word of God" It goes on to say, "and how can they hear without a preacher." Someone must be willing to hear from God, speak His truth, and when that truth is received it results in faith.

Not only do we need to receive in faith, we also have to deliver what we hear by faith. "Let him that prophesies do so according to his **faith**." (Rom. 12:6). So we can see that as it relates to the voice of God faith is important in both receiving and delivering.

We can also see other aspects of faith. Such as, each person receives a measure. (See Rom. 12:3) We can see that it grows. Jesus said, "If you have faith as a mustard seed..:" (See Matt. 17:20) He also said, "According to your faith be it unto you..." (See Matt. 9:29).

This last statement by Jesus is important for us to consider. It confirms for us the reality of God's statement to me, "They hear this way because they were taught to hear a still small voice." Many people underestimate the power of faith as a vehicle of reception. What we experience is directly related to our faith and what we are taught to apply that faith to as truth.

For so long God's people have applied their faith to looking for a still small a voice because it was taught to them by a preacher. Remember, "And how shall they hear without a preacher". This is why listening to the right voice is so important. Listening to a preacher that tells you that you have to accept less than the word of God provides, decreases your chances of experiencing fulfillment. You will only go as far as your faith, "Be it unto you **according to** your faith".

This means you must raise your level of expectation. Many people think that faith and expectation are one and the same. However, they are not. The Bible says, "**Faith** is the substance of things **expected**." Faith is the invisible reality that we desire. Expectation is the vehicle of receiving that desire. God shared this with me as He was teaching me healing.

I had been praying with people with no results. What made it strange was the fact that I felt the power of God on me and I felt it leave me. The recipient also felt the power, but nothing would happen. Not even later in the day or the next day. So I went to God with questions. I said, "What is going on?" He said, "You have to open up their expectation". I had been asking people with injuries if I could pray for them. Apparently, I was not asking the right question or leaving out important information. The Holy Spirit then took me to John 5:6, and reminded me of the question He asked the paralytic. He said to him, "Do you want to be made well". He showed me how all throughout scripture, no one got anything from God that was not expecting to receive something from God.

It was an interesting revelation. I took it upon myself to look up every healing passage in Mark. I discovered that just as God said, there was not one person that received anything from God that was not expecting to receive something. Then I realized that my line of questioning had to change from, "Can I pray for you", to "Can I pray for you, I believe God will heal you." I realized that I needed to give them something to look forward to receiving.

This is a universal truth that includes how we hear from God. If you look at the prophet Samuel in 1 Samuel 3, we see this reality. Samuel thought it was Eli calling his name until Eli opened up his expectation. Once Eli told the young boy what to expect Samuel heard God's voice, for he said to him, "When He calls again". The word "when" is a word that references time. It communicates to Samuel that at some point God is going to speak again. Eli opened up Samuel's expectation!

Looking at this from a more practical standpoint, I urge you to consider your dreams. Have you seriously considered that God may have been speaking to you in one of those "pizza" dreams? More than likely God has been trying to communicate with you just as He was with Samuel, but to no avail. The problem is not that you didn't hear His voice, nor did you purposefully neglected God. You simply didn't know to look for Him to speak.

I have a very dear friend who is always in search of her destiny. What's interesting is the fact that she has had several dreams over a 20 year period with the same theme. Yet, she says that she has not heard from God yet. When I attempted to show her that God was speaking to her in dreams, she blew me off, and said, "That was just a dream". She could not receive His answer because of her lack of expectation that He would actually answer. I suspect that this is the reason so many Christians struggle in their prayer life. Prayer to most people is a chore because they don't actually speak to God with the expectation that He will answer. Expectation is an absolute must in all aspects of our Christian walk.

It is especially true when it comes to hearing the clear voice of God in your life. If you open up your expectation to this reality and apply your faith to it, you will hear God's clear voice. You will find that this is true in every area of your life. What you hear and believe is what you will be open to receive. So be careful how you hear so that you can live in freedom and not by restriction!

16 | How to Exercise Your Ears

There is no doubt in my mind that you are wondering how to get to the unimaginable place that I'm describing. I at one point wondered the same thing. One thing, however, you must keep in mind is the fact that this is a process. That means that you must be committed and willing to sacrifice to receive the benefits of this revelation. Remember, we must **"exercise"** our senses by **"reason of use"**.

This means that we must constantly and consistently expose ourselves to practicing the principles presented. I know that this seems unreasonable to some. Nevertheless, we are not new to the idea of practicing spiritual things. Some years ago a book was written called *Practicing the Presence of God*. It taught principles regarding how to remain engaged in the reality of God's presence. Then we had other books such as Benny Hinn's, *Good Morning Holy Spirit* that grounded us in the reality of God the Holy Spirit as a person we could know intimately. Lately, we have had books on seeing in the spirit. These books provided us with exercises that allowed us to engage the spiritual reality where God dwells. Last, we have such spiritual generals as Prophet Bill Hamon who has proven that spiritual senses can be trained. He has in fact trained thousands of prophets to hear from God.

So the idea of practicing using your spiritual senses should not be strange to you, but welcomed. How can we engage our spiritual ears to hear in the spirit?

First we need to remind ourselves of a few important principles before we get started.

1. **God speaks from His presence.** You will find that God will make you aware of His reality before He speaks.

2. **God gets our attention.** He will allow you to know that He is there and that He wants to speak.

3. **God fills then flows.** This will be especially critical for my prophetic brethren. I cover this is much more detail in my book *God, Is that You, Me, or the Devil?*

4. **God brings us before His throne with worship.** Whenever I hear worship I know God is drawing me near to Himself to speak to me about something. He uses the music to capture my attention and adjust my focus.

5. **It is a process; hence you need to practice listening.** I encourage you to practice by actually learning how to actively listen to others. Listening is listening! If you are not developing a habit of active listening then this particular function of your person (as a whole) will be undeveloped—naturally and spiritually.

Practicing Listening!

The first step in our process is learning how to listen. This means that you must intentionally look for God to speak. You do so by setting your mind on Him!

As stated above, the best way to learn how to listen to God is to learn how to listen to others. Peter provides us with some really great insight into the nature of God. He said that we are liars if we say that we love God but hate man. This communicates a principle. It communicates to us the fact that how we interact with people has an effect on how we interact with God. I believe this principle has a broad application. For instance Jesus said that if we don't forgive others their offense, that He would not forgive us our offenses.

I believe this likewise applies to listening. Listening is a skill that must be mastered. Therefore the best way to exercise our ability to listen is to listen to our spouse, our children, our co-workers, strangers with whom we have the privilege of speaking to.

So after you have gotten your mind focused inward, then listen. The Holy Spirit will guide you into the presence of God. Remember that we come before Him with singing. So you will likely begin to hear a sponta-neous song. If you pay attention you will notice that you have no control of the song. This occurs because it is the Holy Spirit that generates it.

Upon hearing the song tune in deeper by intentionally listening close-ly. After a split second you will notice that the volume is increasing. The more attention you give it, the louder and more distinct it will become.

This should all be done in your quiet time with the Lord. Please re-member that these are exercises aimed at training you to listen intention-ally with your spiritual ears. After you are more comfortable with tuning in, you can go outside of that quiet time. After all, it is the goal of God for you to be available to Him at any time. I can now tune into that spot anytime anywhere, regardless of whom or what is happening around me. That means that I am available if God wants' to speak to me and He does. When He is not speaking to me, He makes sure that my heart has a song to sing.

Again, I generally know that He wants me to tune in because He will stir up a spontaneous song. When I hear the song I tune in and listen.

Learn How to Pray!

One thing that must be important to anyone that hopes to experience hearing the voice of God clearly is prayer. So many times people want to get something for nothing. People like to say salvation is free, and it is. Your admission to the kingdom of God is in fact free, but the things in it have a price. Now I know that the Bible says, "He that did not spare His own Son, but delivered Him up for us all, how shall He not with Him **freely give** us **all things**." (Rom. 8:32) But the word "freely" in that passage is meant to convey the willingness of God to give things to us. John likewise, tells us that if we ask anything according to His will and if we know that He hears us, that we have possession of the things that we asked for. So we know that God is willing and ready to give to us. (See John 5:14)

That however, does not mean that there is not a cost associated with these things. For instance consider that the promise in 1 John 5:14, mentioned above, is contingent on your willingness to believe. We can say the same thing about salvation. We are saved by grace through faith (See Eph. 2:8). So there is a currency associated with obtaining things in the kingdom of God. As we have discussed in a previous chapter, faith is one of them. The other is sacrifice.

Romans 12:1 says, "Present your bodies a living sacrifice, holy acceptable to God, which is your reasonable service." This is a cost, but paying the cost has a reward. For it goes on to say, "That you may be able to prove that good, acceptable, and perfect will of God." So there is a connection between paying the cost of sacrifice and knowing the will of God.

So yes, salvation and access to the kingdom of God is free. And once you are inside you may browse as much as you want. But to take advantage of that access you will need to pay the price of "sacrifice" and "faith!" With these two the world will open up to you.

Pressing Through in Prayer

One of the sacrifices we must learn to make is praying through to the presence of God. Some refer to it as "breaking through" in prayer. Nothing is more discouraging than seeing Christians who can't spend 30 good minutes in prayer. Jesus once challenged the disciples about this issue in the Garden of Gethsemane. He said to them, "Could you not watch one hour?" He doesn't stop there He also said, "Watch and pray lest you enter into temptation." This infers that prayer is a type of spiritual warfare. The last thing that He said was the most important for this discussion. He said, "The spirit is willing, but the flesh is weak." This means that there is a part of us that wants to pray, and there is a part of us that struggles to endure the process. (See Matt. 26:40-43)

Why is this important? One thing that makes this so important is found in Jesus' initial statement, "Watch and pray." This statement, more specifically the word "watch", tells us that we have access to insight in prayer. That insight is a strategy to your success in any area of your life. It also teaches us that God speaks to us in a place of prayer.

Just consider that the Bible says that Peter encountered a vision while he was in prayer (See Acts 10:9). Likewise Jesus says to Ananias that a man named Paul was praying when he saw in a vision a man coming in to him and restoring his sight (Acts 9:11-12). So prayer is a strategic place of warfare for the believer. It is the vehicle of insight.

But we must also know that it is a place of warfare! This is why Jesus encouraged them to pray lest they fall into temptation. This is an admonishment to spend time in the presence of God. Might I again remind you that God speaks to us from His presence.

Even in Elijah's experience on Mount Horeb we see that God's voice was clearly heard coming out of His presence. For example, when God spoke to him in the cave it says, "The word of the Lord **came to** Elijah (1 Kings 19:9). This means that God spoke from His presence. Likewise when he heard the clear voice of God it says, "And the Lord **passed by**." (1 Kings 19:11) It was after the Lord's presence is introduced in verse 11 that the "sudden voice" was heard. The only time the voice of God was unclear was in the still small voice experience. That was directly related to the fact that Elijah was not in the place where God was speaking. He was outside of the presence of God. But as soon as he entered the presence he found access to insight!

The Process of Pressing In

If we need to get into the presence of God to hear Him clearly and prayer is our door to Him, and our flesh is resistant to prayer, what are we to do? How do we press into the presence?

What I am going to share with you is something that God taught me that allows me to walk in this place with Him. It is a process of prayer that will take you into a deeper manifestation of the presence of God. It is meant to help you learn the process, but ultimately the goal is learning how to master the process so that you always have access to him. It is not a daily process but from time to time you will discover that there are seasons when you must put it into practice. I also forewarn you that you will experience warfare! You will experience a dying of your flesh as the enemy does everything possible to keep you out of this place. So make up your mind to press your way and endure or you will be just like the disciples...asleep!

Three Levels in Prayer

God taught me that there were three levels to prayer. There is the body level, the soul level, and the spirit level. Each of these are layers of prayer that we experience. To understand what I saying I am going to break down a familiar passage that God used to teach me this principle. That passage is Luke 8:40-48, the story of the woman with the issue of blood.

I want you to take out a piece of paper and draw three circles on it. Draw one big circle then draw a smaller circle inside of the bigger circle. Then draw a third circle inside of the second circle. If done properly you should have three rings. This symbolizes the three layers of prayer. The outer most ring represents the crowd present in the story. The inner ring represents the disciples. And the inner most ring represents Jesus. Next I want you to take an object and place it outside of the outer most ring. This object represents the woman with the issue of blood.

Each of these elements represents something in the story. The crowd represents the physical forces that fight to keep you away from the goal, the presence of God. It also represents the crowdedness of the day or mind. The disciples represent the conscience and our own sense of righteousness or wretchedness. Many times the disciples were seen pushing people away and restricting access to the Jesus. They did this to the children (See Matt. 19:13-15). They are seen doing this to the Syro-Phoenicians woman whose daughter had a demon (See Matt. 15:22-23). And they are seen exhibiting self-righteous behavior regarding the man who was casting out demons who did not follow them (See Luke 9:49). They are a shadow type of those who do not really understand God's forgiveness, acceptance, and unconditional love. They were self-righteous. Last there is the center, the place where Jesus is and of course He represents the presence of God.

So get the picture. This woman needs to get through a crowd, past the disciples and into the presence of God. She has to get past physical challenges, the loud voices of the crowd, and condemnation to get to Jesus. Is it starting to sound familiar yet! Most people come to prayer and fight the physical challenges of sleep, tiredness, or just waiting. Then if we can get past our physical hindrances we find ourselves struggling with a wayward mind that is filling with thoughts and ideas. Then when we finally get close enough to experience the presence the last war begins and we struggle with feelings of unworthiness. For most people this is where the battle is lost.

Most people experience a sense of incredible guilt over the sins that they have committed throughout the day. Sometimes it is something as simple as an argument over something silly. This tells me that people really need to understand forgiveness and grace.

One of the things that frustrate me is how the Church constantly and consistently misapplies truth. Today we have Christians who live on the extreme of today's grace teachings. Some call it hyper-grace. It is a teaching spawned from those who are tired of what they call "legalistic" teaching. They do not teach sin, but the teaching is often misunderstood as a license to sin. This happens simply because we have a faulty understanding of God. We think that God's new things replaces God's old things. But Isaiah 28:10 tells us that truth is built precept upon precept or principle upon principle. Likewise Jesus refers to Himself as a builder. Paul calls Him the Chief cornerstone (See Eph. 2:20). You should know that God is not doing away with the standard of holiness, but balancing our understanding of it. First He taught us what holiness was. Now He is teaching us how to live it. Living holy does not mean that we live perfect lives that make us worthy of the presence of God. It is living with the goal of being separated for God's glory. Grace is there when we miss the mark. It is the thing that allows God to say, "I know you did it. I forgive you. You can always come to my throne of grace in time of need". That need in the passage is sin, what we receive in return is forgiveness. (See Heb. 4:16)

So as we press into His presence it is ever important that we first aim to live holy, second that we realize that when we fail we are forgiven. Understanding this will immediately take the sting out of condemnation.

As for pressing into the presence in prayer know that there is a goal to this process. That goal is to break you down. There is an interesting aspect of the story to consider. This woman started out walking but eventually found herself low enough to the ground to touch the hem of Jesus' garment. The process of getting into His presence brought her low. Furthermore it was in the place of humility that she got what she needed.

This takes me back to the issue of transparency. Sometimes we come before God with what I call the "representative". He or she is usually the version of our self that we deem acceptable to God. This means we are inclined to pray with our heads and not with our hearts. We often work hard to make sure we say the right thing, quote the right scripture, have repented of any sin, etc. For this reason a lot of people cringe at the idea of praying for an hour or more. When I tell people I once prayed for eight hours they always wonder what I talked about for eight hours. I usually ask them if they have ever been on the phone for more than an hour. I ask them this because the reality is that there is not much of a difference between talking to God and talking to people. The only reason we talk to people for an hour or more on the phone is because we talk to them from our heart and not from our head. And we can talk to them from our heart because we have invested the time in getting to know what that person likes to talk about. Likewise we feel comfortable to share our heart.

Prayer is the same way. The process of pressing into His presence helps us get to the "heart" that is in us so that we can communicate in prayer from that place. The Bible says that the issues of life flow from our heart, not our head (See Pro. 4:23). God is interested in knowing what is on your heart. And trust me, this process eliminates pride and humbles us. That means that your heart may spew forth pain, anger, frustration, joy and anything else that needs to be resolved through prayer.

One thing I have come to value about my relationship with God is that He allows me to be me. I can be angry like Jonah, I can be hurt or weak, or I can be frustrated and He is right there to speak to me and resolve my issues. I can be transparent with Him. So the process breaks down the performance that often happens when we come to prayer and allows us to be transparent and vulnerable.

The Misconception About Prayer

Often people are intimidated at the thought of being in prayer for hours. This feeling of intimidation is rooted in the misunderstanding about what being in prayer entails.

Being in prayer does not mean talking for hours. Prayer is a combination of expressions like speaking and singing. When Jesus taught the disciples how to pray the very first thing that He taught them was the element of worship. He said, "When you pray say our Father which is in heaven **hallowed be thy name.**" He taught them that they needed to approach the throne by acknowledging God's greatness. The Bible says, "Enter into His gates with thanksgiving, and into His courts with praise, be thankful to Him and bless His holy name." (Ps. 100:4)

So prayer also involves worship. When a person tells you that they have been in prayer for five hours very rarely does that mean that the talked for five hours. Some of that time was spent singing to God and worshiping Him. Then there are other times when a person may decide to spend time just thanking Him for things in their life. Yet at other times within the prayer a person may intercede for others. My point is prayer consist of various elements.

One of those elements is listening. Some of those hours in prayer involve you listening to God. This book is about one of the ways that He may speak to you in prayer. We have already taken a sneak peek into the pray time of Peter and Paul and seen where their prayer time involved hearing from God. Each of them heard from God during their time of prayer. So as you venture into pressing into the presence God just know that you can hear also.

Pressing in Prayer Exercise

1. **Come to prayer and sit patiently waiting.** You may sing or sit quietly until the Holy Spirit inspires a song to sing. This can be practiced anywhere and at any time. I am often filled with a song while out and about. Remember this is the precursor to His voice (You may also find it useful to put on a worship CD and sing along)

2. **Worship from the heart not from the head.** One thing about worship you will soon discover is that it is either coming from the heart or the head. Every Sunday people gather in a building and treat worship as a preliminary exercise to preaching. Many men and women of God have completely lost the ability to communicate the value of genuine worship. So in your initial attempt at pressing into God's presence you may find yourself in a place such as the woman with the issue of blood, in the crowd. This means that after sometime you will get tired and weary of worshipping. This is a sign that it is not coming from your heart but is being done as a formality. This will not take you into the presence. You may even get so weary that you stop worshipping. But if you wait until you get to the end of yourself, you will find a song. That song is the song that the Holy Spirit will inspire inside of you. When you hear your heart singing, join in.

3. **Keep pressing**. It won't be long before you attract the disciples. At this point you may experience a great deal of spiritual warfare. This means that Satan is working really hard to hinder your efforts at pressing in. Your mind may begin to fill with wayward thoughts, and even accusatory thoughts about your failures. You may also hear discouraging thoughts suggesting that you are being foolish

or that it won't happen, or that you are not good enough. This all happens in the "crowd" and with "the disciples".

The other thing that you may encounter is the all too common sudden feeling of overwhelming tiredness. This usually leads to falling asleep and is preceded by a feeling of heaviness. This oppressive feeling is a spirit at work trying to discourage you from praying. I use to experience this when sitting during prayer or as I read my Bible. That being the case I opted for standing and walking during prayer. I was sure that this would prove valuable. But it didn't! This is how I learned that I was really in a spiritual battle. It was so strange. There I was standing and walking back in forth when this heavy feeling of sleepiness would came over me. And many of you have experienced the same thing. This is the reason!

Remember one of Satan's primary goals is to "distract" you and cause you to lose focus. He does not want God to guide your mind into His presence and hell will create all types of distractions physical and spiritual to stop you.

4. **Don't freak out!** One thing that you will encounter as you breakthrough in prayer is the presence of God. When you get past the crowd, and past the disciples and your mind gets focused, you will experience God is a very real way. You will find yourself in an overwhelming place of peace. In this place God may begin to speak or bring you into visions. That being said please don't freak out and start crying, shaking, OMG'ing, and the like. Remember you are coming into His presence to commune and share time with Him. So don't make the moment awkward. The only reason this is strange to you is because you are not used to it.

I always find it strange when people say that they had a visitation from God. It makes me say to God, "Did you go somewhere that I don't know about?" The reality is that God is never a visitor and He is always present. The problem is that most of the time we are more immersed in earthly things that make us numb to spiritual things. The thought of God visiting once or twice a year is scary to me. I have gotten so use to experiencing Him every single day, and not in theory, but tangibly. If you follow what I am showing you, you will be able to say the same thing. So don't freak out, God wants to talk to you!

The most important thing to take away from this section is to remain open. That means that you should not treat this as some type of pattern that you use every time you enter into a time of prayer. The ideas presented are principles to be mastered or incorporated into your everyday life. I do not walk through this process every day. I have learned to recognize the sensation of God filling me and I likewise recognize the song of the Lord in my heart. I know that it means that God wants to guide my mind into focusing on His presence so that He can speak to me. That spontaneous worship can happen and does happen at any time. Likewise I don't always have to pass the disciples. I understand forgiveness and I live a lifestyle of confession and repentance, so Satan has no power over my conscience. I haven't experience shame and guilt in many years!

Everything presented is aimed at helping you to learn how to live with an ongoing experience of God's presence. That being said, the other most consistent thing you will experience is warfare. Oh how I wish this were not so, but it is! You will have times when hell fights you to such a degree that your senses get dulled or dimmed. When this happens it is time to fight. How do you fight? Go through the process to breakthrough in prayer. This may take minutes or sometimes it can take hours. But if you press your way past the crowd and the disciples, you will breakthrough to His presence and the voice of God will be clear again

17 | Conclusion

In conclusion, I pray that I was able to inspire in you a deeper yearning for God's voice. The Church has been great at developing feelers and seers. Now it is time for the Church to realize that it is also possible to hear God's voice clearly.

That being said, I find it equally important to stress the idea that we must be open for God to use whatever sense He deems necessary at that moment. It has been my experience, that God will use the sense or senses that are most appropriate for communicating a particular truth. For instance, sometimes a picture is worth a thousand words. However, there are some deeper truths that a picture will never be able to capture. Sometimes you will find that He uses two or even all three senses in communicating to you.

Here's a personal example. After many nights of peaceful rest, my three-year-old daughter suddenly began calling me frantically in the middle of the night. At first it was just to use the bathroom. Being the good daddy that I am, I jumped out of bed and quickly went to her aid. Then one night she called to me frantically and when I went to check on her she simply wanted a hug. And of course I gave her a hug. I was a little annoyed, but love compelled me to meet the need.

These frantic calls in the middle of the night continued for a few weeks. It happened so often that I decided to seek God about what was happening. His response to me was precious. As I sought an answer I had a sudden sense that God was saying two things. One, He was showing me that a real Father responds to the cry of His child, speaking of Himself. The second thing He was saying to me is, "You used to come when I called in the middle of the night!"

It was God's last statement that really struck me at my core. I don't have a regular time of study, prayer, and worship like most people. I have learned to come at the beckoning of God. This means that I have heard the call many times in the wee hours of the morning. Eventually, however, a time came when I stopped responding to the midnight calls and I fell into a natural routine of praying in the morning.

Now I know this does not seem like a bad thing to many of those reading. However, God has trained me to live by His calling. So when He calls I come.

He trained me this way so that I do not fall into a normal routine of hearing from Him only at certain times. He wants me available and sensitive to His leading at every moment. So His statement to me spoke volumes.

That being said, this is a great example of being open for God to speak in a way that He deems appropriate for the situation. God could have told me in a voice, dream, or vision. It would have been just as easy to receive. Nevertheless, He decided to make it personal by allowing me to experience a situation that helped me to identify with how He felt. In doing so He drove home His point. So as you seek to encounter Him be open. I did not write this book for you to dictate to God how to speak to you. As you can see God speaks to me in various ways.

The point of this book is to assist you with developing your spiritual hearing. There are likewise, other great books to assist you with developing your sense of "feeling" and "seeing" as well. I highly encourage you to invest in those books as well.

I have learned to dwell with God as a man would His spouse. Every married couple understands that sometimes communication can be done verbally and nonverbally. Sometimes a gesture is all you need. You will find the same is true in your relationship with God. There will be times when you hear His clear voice, and other times when He simply gestures. Overtime and after investing in a relationship with Him you will become absolutely comfortable with either.

It All Comes Down to This

Finally as I close, I want to say that the principles of disobedience, lack of focus, spiritual warfare, and pain all apply to any of the ways in which we experience God's voice. Adhering to these principles will make hearing better, feeling stronger, and seeing clearer. I initially thought that the dream was just about hearing. Then I came to understand that it was about all of our senses.

To really cement these ideas in my life God has taken me through the four hindrances to clearer hearing. I have experienced a dulling of my senses – all of them! As I applied these principles I started to realize that not only did I hear better, but my perception was stronger and my visions and dreams were clearer.

A Word About Flow

The Bible says in John 7:38, "Whoever believes in Me, as the scriptures has said, out of his heart will flow rivers of living waters. This He spoke of the Holy Spirit." Jesus tells us that there should be a flow of the Spirit of God in our life. But somehow we have gotten to a place of seeing the Spirit of God trickling in our life.

Having been in the flow and having been in the place of seeing a trickle, I understand the cause. God has taught me that a trickle is a sign of an obstruction. That is when we need to pull aside and do an assessment of our self. That is what the principles of this book are for – self-assessment. They are to help you identify the reasons for the trickling of God's voice in your life.

Every preacher, teacher, or intercessor knows what I mean. There are times when we get up to preach, teach, or pray and the Spirit of God flows out of us like water. Other times we seem dry and He seems hindered or restricted from flowing. My advice as I conclude is that you take time to assess your spiritual state. This idea of self-assessment is not new to Christians. Even Paul says that we need to examine ourselves as to whether or not we are in the faith..." (See 2 Cor. 13:5) The overall principle of the passage is that we all need to take time to do a spiritual check-up.

Again this is not a foreign concept to us. Just consider this example. If you own a vehicle you know that sometimes mechanical issues occur that hinder the vehicle from operating smoothly. When this happens we know that it is time to take it off the road and into the shop. In the shop the mechanic runs test called diagnostic . This simply means that they are doing an assessment. To do so they use a set of standards. The point is that when things do not flow smoothly, whether it is your vehicle, your health, or even your career, an assessment is needed.

You should do the same in your spiritual life. Set aside time to assess your spiritual condition so that you can live in the flow of the Holy Spirit and not operate from the trickle. You can hear the voice of God clearly in your life.

One Final Word

The last thing that I want to say before I close out this document is that it is important to couple learning to hear with learning to discern. So many books on the subject of God's voice spend a great deal of time outlining principles for hearing. Very few, however, make any real effort at engaging the subject of discernment. In my chapter "The Voice I Hear or the Voice I Know", I shed just a little light on the subject of how to be certain when God speaks to you.

But I have another book that is written exclusively on that subject of discerning God's voice from all others. It is called, *"God, Is that You, Me, or the Devil?" How to confidently know God's voice.* In this book you will find detailed information about the voice of God. It was my aim to answer that question and I believe I accomplished that mission.

In it I discuss the differences between the voice of God and the leading of the Holy Spirit; How to be led by the Holy Spirit; The differences between your voice, God's voice, and Satan's voice; What God talks about (to protect us from wayward conversations); What is the fruit of those conversations with God. I even cover how you may experience the voice of God when He begins to speak to you and so much more. I left no stone unturned. In it I cover everything you need to know to have confidence in learning to hear from God.

It was derived from one experience that took many years of training from God. He taught me everything you will read in those pages and I promise you the insight contained therein will take you into a deeper place in Christ. And most importantly it does not contain my opinion on the subject, but each chapter is steeped in scriptures. That means that you can trust it as a way of measuring your experience.

So if you enjoyed this book. I invite you to purchase your copy of _"God, Is that You, Me, or the Devil"_ and get solid answers to that most nagging question.

Bonus Chapter

In the following pages you will find a bonus chapter from my forthcoming book. Please enjoy learning what the Bible reveals to us about the ways God speaks.

You are likewise invited to check out the links on the very last page of this book. I post weekly teachings/sermons on my **Facebook** page and **YouTube** channel that will bless you. You are also invited to follow me on **Periscope** and **Twitter** under my name Kevin Winters. If the information in this book has blessed you then you will be blessed by the many other free teachings/sermons you will find there. Thanks you for reading!

18 | Bonus Chapter: *Ways God Speaks*

From the Upcoming Book - *God, Is that You, Me, or the Devil?*

Jesus said *"My sheep hear my Voice"* (*John 10:27, NKJV*). If we are not hearing the voice God, this statement suggests to us that the problem is not a transmitter issue. It is a receiver issue. For this statement is an emphatic statement not a passive one. Jesus is not saying My sheep hear My voice. He's saying MY sheep HEAR ME! The stranger's voice they won't hear or give attention to, because they are not familiar with that voice. There is no comfort to them in the sound of the voice of a stranger.

I was teaching my children this concept and I was teaching it from the position of fear. And you know what I mean—I was teaching them that they should to be careful because the devil can speak to them also. As I was teaching them my parental version of the word, the Lord interrupted the conversation and said rather forcefully, "MY sheep hear MY voice. But wanting to protect my children from deception, I continued to teach them my version but I adjusted my message slightly, when again the Lord interrupted me and said," MY SHEEP, HEAR MY VOICE!!!

So I began to instruct them about how to study God in the scriptures and encouraged them to continue to seek the Lord. I left it in the in the hands of the Shepherd and made myself available to help them discern.

Why am I starting with this particular truth? I know that God's voice is not the only voice we literally hear. Satan and his cohorts speak to us as well. However it is important for us to know that Jesus' voice is distinct and different. Also, real Christians do not need to worry themselves with Satan's voice because the reality is Jesus says that Satan's voice is one that "HIS SHEEP WON'T" follow! Therefore, you do not need to be overly concerned or consumed with the fear of being deceived. You will have seasons like Jesus in the wilderness when you will be tempted but, but you will know that is it is not God speaking because Satan voice will always point you to YOU. Jesus leads us to Himself. One truth you will see me presented often is that _"the spirit of prophecy is the testimony of Jesus Christ"_ (Rev. 19:10). I am going to drill this truth into you because it is the safe guard against deception.

The understanding that Jesus points us to Himself will help us as we move forward in discussing how He speaks to us. It will also give us the peace we need to position ourselves to hear Him in ways that some consider controversial, even though they are biblical. The controversy is spawned by the fear of deception, and the many examples of those deceived in such ways. I have to point out however, that if we look as the David Koreshs, Daddy Graces, and many other self-proclaimed Christ who claim that they came to such an idea through a voice, dream or vision, we will see that they violated a basic truth. That truth again is that God testifies and points us to Himself. "If we draw near to Him, He WILL DRAW near to us", and that can only be accomplished if you walk in the safety of this basic truth.

Now that we know that Jesus says that "His sheep hear His voice" and that He points us to Himself, we need to discuss how He speaks to His sheep. How does God communicate with us? That is the question we will answer in the pages to follow.

Audible Voice

One of the most incredible ways in which God may choose to speak to you is in an audible voice. This mode of communication is one of the most constant and visible attributes of how God communicated with mankind. And as I pointed out in chapter 1, this is how He spoke to mankind until after the fall. After the fall we can see a progressive falling away and eventually, we see that God and man have a silent period.

So God speaks in an audible voice, and I believe that He desires to do so more often today. Some would describe it as a still small voice deep down inside. And usually to hear it you have to sit still and be quiet for hours waiting to hear a faint sound in your heart. This is not what God desires. I go into much more detail in my chapter on "Hindrances to Hearing". But God's voice is a voice, that can be heard clearly and it is not a still small voice. This is an important truth to accept, because it will help you open up your faith to receive what He really wants to do.

The reason you hear a still small voice is because this is the teaching that your faith has been applied to, and so it is what you have come to expect to hear. However, if you open your faith to the reality that God speaks in an audible voice, you will find that it is much easier to hear.

God does not want you to strain to hear His voice. He desires fellowship with you and He has made it easy for that to happen. Also, this popular teaching violates the basics of biblical interpretation. One should never develop a doctrine around one passage of scripture. You will never see the term "still small voice" ever again in scripture when God is speaking, but you will see God speaking in a clear voice in thousands of passages. And it is consistently seen in the Old Testament and the New Testament.

I can recall a particular time in my life when God spoke to me the first time in an audible voice. I had been working in the file room for years before I was detailed to another office as an office assistant. The detail was to be thirty days, but turned into three years. While in the job, I did a lot of small tasks and menial work, but I believed that the will of God was for me to always do my work as unto the Lord. And that's what I did.

To make a long story short, one day as I sat in prayer before God, I heard a voice clearly say, "You are going to get a job offer tomorrow, do not turn it down". The moment I heard it I knew that it was the Lord, but I have to admit, it was a bit startling. I've had many experiences with the Lord but this one was new and different for me.

In the middle of the next day my boss approached me with a question about the job that God had told me was coming. I quickly found out why He said not to refuse the offer. I was at the time in a permanent employee status and the new job required me to go into temporary status. This meant that after a certain time my position would be terminated and I would be out of a job.

I wish I could tell you that I was obedient, but I became afraid and the opportunity passed. The job was given to another co-worker and one month later it was converted into a permanent position. This could have been a perfect story, but the good thing is approximately 6 months later the offer was made again and I accepted.

I also want us to understand that in the Bible people heard the audible voice of God in different ways. It was obvious that Adam, Eve, Cain, and Moses heard an external audible voice. Phillip is one of our New Testament examples of God speaking in an audible external voice in Act 8:29. But there were some people who actually heard the voice of God internally in a dream or vision. Such was the case with Abraham when God gave him a dream that his descendants would be as innumerable as the sand on sea Genesis 40:23. Peter in Acts 10:13 is another example of God speaking to us in an internal audible voice. Peter says he saw a great sheet let down from heaven and he heard a voice say, "Rise Peter Kill and eat".

So as you open up your faith to receive the audible voice of God, just understand that it may happen in one of the two ways.

Dreams and Visions

One of the other ways, in which, God may choose to speak to you is in a dream or a vision. Dreams and visions are mental images impressed into the mind during a conscious or unconscious state. The major difference between the two is that dreams are received during a sleeping state, while visions can be received while sleeping or awake.

Dreams and visions are fascinating to a lot of people and God uses them to speak to people for many different reasons. Some are used to provide direction as with Abraham when he left his family for the land that God would show him (Gen. 12:1). Or he may use them to challenge our perspectives and mindsets, such as He did when He helped Peter accept the gentiles (Acts 10:11-16) and Joseph when he was going to put away Mary for what he thought was an illegitimate conception (Matt. 1:20). Sometimes He will show us our future as he did with Joseph (Gen. 37:5-11), and to warn us as he did with the king who was going to sleep with Abraham's wife (Gen. 20:1-7). No matter how He chooses to deliver His message to you, just know that it is important.

Vision of Jesus

I have had many visions and dreams. One of my favorite occurred as I was writing this book. God initially told me that He wanted this book written within a certain time frame. Therefore, He impressed upon me often to write and I did. At some point in the process however, when I started writing a particular chapter, I just could not figure out how to address the subject. Knowing what to do and explaining it to someone else are quite different. I had written maybe two paragraphs of that chapter when I finally said, " Lord this is not working."

In frustration I asked the Lord how He wanted me to approach this subject? I told Him I really needed His help with this subject, because it was difficult to explain. Then I sat in my chair and waited. Then after 30 minutes or so, I got up and waited and waited. Later that night I returned to my chair and was waiting some more when all of a sudden, I see a figure in an illuminated white gown fly into what I assume was the room I was in. He was at distance and he had something in his hand. It was a rolled up piece of paper. As I was looking He unrolled it and there was writing on it. I could see the words but not clearly. The figure smiled at me and then flew away.

It did not dawn on me until the next day what was on that piece of paper. It was a vision from God giving me what I needed to write these chapters that I was struggling to complete. Once I accepted the vision the words for those chapters began to poor out me like rivers of living water.

This is an example of how God interacts with us in a vision to help us accomplish His will.

Vision of the Wolf Lamb

Sometimes God speaks to us in visions to get us to accept truth. This was the case in this next story. I actually had this vision at a stoplight.

I was infatuated with a young lady at the time that I had only seen walking around on the job. This young lady was beautiful and friendly and she carried herself with such dignity and respect. She seemed meek and was always very polite. However, this was FAR from the truth.

I was so captivated by this woman that I had to talk to God about her. So one day as I sat at a stoplight I said, "Lord, what's up with the light skinned girl on the job". No sooner I said that, I saw in my mind a picture of a sheep and as I kept looking at it, the sheep began to turn into a wolf. This vision was completely contrary to what I had observed. I never saw or heard of anything that indicated that this woman was dangerous. So I asked the question again. And again I saw a clear picture of a sheep that turned into a wolf.

Having heard from the Lord I took the vision for what it was worth left this woman alone. Sometime went by and I was detailed to the position I spoke of in the chapter, and guess who was there? Yep, this same woman! It was not even a day before I discovered that she was extremely promiscuous, a habitual liar, and a drunk. What happened to the nice young lady I had met? This was definitely a case of Dr. Jekyll and Mrs. Hyde!

This woman almost caused me to fall into sin, but God prepared me by giving me a simple image with a vital truth attached. And No, I was not in a trance during the vision. This is what is known as a mental vision and it happens to many of you more often than you may realize. After reading this book I pray that you will begin to recognize this more often.

Vision for Warfare and Intercession

Sometimes God has a very specific reason for giving you a dream or vision. Spiritual warfare is one such occasion. God will sometimes show you how the enemy is operating against a church, organization, or individual.

We see this happen in 2 Kings 6:17-20 when Elisha is caught between a rock and a hard spot. He has been revealing the King of Assyria's plan to attack the King of Israel. The King of Assyria is perplexed by who is betraying him and revealing his plans. One of his servants tells him that the prophet in Israel is telling the kings secret. The king of Assyria decides that he is going to capture Elisha and kill him so he goes by night to the place where his lodging. When Elisha and his servant awaken they realize that they are completely surrounded by soldiers. Elisha's servant then becomes overwhelmed with fear and Elisha prays a simple prayer. *"Lord, open his eyes that he might see"* (verse 16). And God answered Elisha's prayer and opened the servant's eyes to the spirit realm. When his eyes opened he saw that there were angels all about protecting them. This allowed Elisha to divert the attack and deliver the enemy into the hands of the king of Israel.

On one occasion as I was in prayer I saw a vision of a church with a large dark, 200 foot principality standing over it. This being was armed with a sword. He drew the sword and struck the church and divided it in half. Soon after the hands of the Lord grabbed the side of the church and put it back together and it looked as if nothing had occurred.

This vision revealed that a principality of division was starting an attack against this particular church. This was God telling me how He needed me to intercede in prayer for this church.

On another occasion, God revealed the enemy's plan against a Bible study group that I was a part of. This was a mighty group of multi-denominational people who got together every week for prayer and to study the word. One day as we were in prayer I saw in a vision four evil spirits sitting on the counter behind us. They were canvassing the group looking for the weak person in the group. Once they found their victim they began to move in, but not all at once. One would open the door for the next. They were quite systematic and organized in executing their plan. After the last one moved into position the Bible study suffered chaos and soon the drama killed the group.

After the time of prayer I told the vision to the group, but they did not take it to heart. I think they were a little put off by the fact that I saw evil spirits. But anyway, it was not long after that one of the women started having romantic feelings, or should I say lustful feelings, for one of the teachers. This led to chaos, which led to gossip and all of a sudden this group that had 15-20 persons in attendance every week praying and interceding for everything possible, was down to 5-6 people every week. God gave them fair warning, but they did not hear. I will admit, that looking back, I should have presented the vision with more wisdom. I was young and inexperienced then, but now I can see how important wisdom is when administering such information.

The Most Beautiful Dream

God also uses dreams to provide us with direction. This is a dream that came at a time in my life before I received Christ as my Savior. The beauty of this dream is that God tried to communicate with me even though I didn't know Him. But the dream clearly shows that He watches over us, even the sinners.

My first couples of years in high school were really boring and uneventful. I spent a great deal of time desiring to be recognized and not get lost in the vast sea of people. When I got to the eleventh grade I discovered something fascinating about myself. I discovered that I loved poetry and that I could rap. This began a new chapter in my life and changed my status as a student.

I loved my new talent and I worked very hard to be the best rapper the world would ever hear. This was to be my career path and I would pursue it until I got what I was after. That meant school did not matter, and so I did just enough to get by. It was ny goal upon graduation to move to New York to pursue my dream.

Then it happened. I dreamed that I was coming up from and underground metro system in New York City. When I got to the top of the staircase all I could see was the entire city of New York made of the most beautiful crystal. I mean it was absolutely fascinating. I still remember how real that dream felt. I could hardly believe it was a dream. The crystal city was the dead give-away.

It would be a few years before I would receive the interpretation of that dream. The dream was an attempt by God to communicate a very important truth about the direction I was headed. In the dream the rising staircase was a depiction of my success in the rap industry. The crystal city communicated the beauty and fragile nature of the dream. One day God finally spoke to me about the dream and He said that it would have only taken a stone to bring my fragile world to an end.

I'm so glad God saved me from going in that direction. He tried to warn me about me direction but I was not able to hear Him. Thank God for His mercy.

Revealing the Heart

Sometimes God uses dreams and visions to reveal our heart when we are stuck in certain patterns of life. For a long time I was timid about displaying anger. I had seen some things in my childhood that left me angry and even after I got saved I worked hard to avoid being in situations where I might get angry. This meant I worked at avoiding confrontations.

So I started talking to the Lord about how to be free to be angry, but not sin. One day as I was walking to the mall I got another mental image. This time however, it was an image of the Incredible Hulk. God was showing me that I was afraid of the monster that I thought might manifest in time of stress. He then began to assure me that He had done the work to free me from my past and that anger was an emotion that I could now control. After this discussion I went on to have healthy confrontations with people that did not involve me becoming violent. I was free.

One thing that you may hear as you open yourself up to receive from God through dreams and visions is that the devil might speak to you. You will also hear that dreams can come from the busyness of the day or issues on your mind. These are both true. Ecclesiastics 5:3 says," *for a dream comes through much activity*".

While I understand their concerns, I tell people all dreams are important even though they are not all from God. If the devil has an issue inside of you and your flesh is struggling with something, then it will manifest in your dreams. Why should you care? These types of dreams assist you in knowing how you should pray and what issues are going on in your heart.

For example, for a couple of years I would have reoccurring dreams about a former girlfriend who made life a living hell. In the dreams I was always doing something violent to her, such as pushing her off the top bunk bed onto the floor. After sometime passed I started to realize that I never grieved the pain that she caused me during the relationship. I was still angry in my heart and it was manifesting in my dreams.

Not long after, I attended a youth retreat and the Spirit of God started moving and dealing with people, and I sensed that this was the perfect time to release this issue to God. So I walked up front with just a tear or two, but by time I hit the floor I was sobbing uncontrollably and I felt all that pain from five years prior that I had bottled up inside of me. I was completely surprised and I did not expect that to happen. After I gave the pain to the Lord I felt much better and I have never had a dream like that again.

I have also had demonic dreams as well. However, I need to tell you that the type of dream I am about to describe is not likely to happen to you. This happened in my life as the gift of discerning of spirits was just beginning to operate. If anyone has this gift you will know what I mean when I say it was not a pleasant introduction to the gift.

I had been having a great year and the Lord was moving in my life in a mighty way. I was witnessing to everyone even my bosses. I had a booming Bible study on the job and prophecy and revelation were flowing regularly. I was wreaking havoc on the kingdom of darkness.

This resulted in a dream. In this dream I saw myself run up to a woman to cast the demon out of her. As I raised my hand to cast it out she turned around and I heard a creepy voice that was not in the dream say, "You don't know who you are dealing with". This stunned me into waking up. When I opened my eyes there was a large dark presence standing over top of me staring angrily down at me as I lay on my bed. So I got up on my bed, looked it in the eyes, (yes it was that large), and told it, "No, You don't know who you're dealing with". Then I rebuked it in the name of Jesus and it left.

This may scare some of you but this is not likely to happen. This was a training period of my life and while I did not enjoy these experiences, I did come to KNOW the reality of the POWER in the NAME of JESUS. They really do flee at that name.

So unless God gives you certain gifts you may never have this type of encounter. Even if you do have such an encounter, rebuke it and go back to sleep.

Sometimes demonic dreams are more subtle. In fact, at the conclusion of writing the first draft of this book I felt a presence fill the air of my bedroom as I was going to bed. It was fear and I could literally sense it in the air as an overwhelming fear. That night as I slept I had a dream about how traditional religious people, to include friends and family, would reject the book. It also attempted to torment me throughout the next day, but I exposed it, rebuked it and the presence left and so did the thoughts and dreams.

These are my personal stories, but the Bible is full of stories of God speaking in dreams and visions.

Impressions

This is probably the most common experience among Christians and occasionally non-Christians. It is usually characterized by the popular clichés "something told me" and "I had a feeling."

Impressions are intuitive feelings, senses, or an inner perceptions or a sudden awareness felt deep within the being of an individual. Impressions may come to us as light as a flash of thought or as strong as an urge. However they may come to us we can be certain that what we perceive is spiritual in nature. This is the most popular form of communication with the spirit world. Even the psychics and the New Age materials refer to the intuitive feeling.

What does this mean to the believer? It means that we must learn how to recognize God, which is the purpose of this book.

I find this particular method of communication very re-assuring. It seems to provide the greatest sense of security. Just consider how many times you have sensed something and ignored it only to find out later that it was true. For instance many of you have known that someone was lying to you. You can't explain it; you just knew deep inside that something wasn't right. I once heard a character on television make this statement. "I trust my intuition, and my intuition doesn't trust you." This seems to sum up this idea.

Some of us refer to this as our knower or the leading of the Spirit. However you may refer to it, it is a good method for measuring the validity of the other three communication methods. If fact, when I am uncertain I weigh the voice against my knower. If I have an unmistakable "knowing" I know I'm good to go.

The hardest thing about this method is learning how to subject our rational minds so that we can trust our inner senses. Also, this method as do all the others, though not to the same extent, require us to make the distinction between what is the Spirit and what is our own imaginations and desires. Some people are prone to projecting what they want as what they sense God is saying. Such as the many prophets who prophesied that President Obama would not receive a second term. Some of them claim to have had dreams and visions, but really it was just what they wanted to see happen manifesting to their hearts. This is why checking the "knower" is valuable.

The Bible says that "the word of God divides between soul and spirit" (Heb. 4:12). It makes the distinction between what is us and what is God. The best examples of this concept that I have heard was a teaching on the voice of God by a prophet who said, that you could liken impressions to those things we experience in the conscience. In our conscience there is no sentence structure as with the audible voice. There are no words, just a sense of right and wrong.

There a lot of examples in the scriptures as well regarding impressions and the many ways we may experience God moving on our inner man.

Perception

One way we might experience an impression as seen in the scriptures is perception. When God is communicating with us we may perceive something. When faced with a storm Paul says, "*Men I PERCIEVE that this voyage will end in disaster...*" (Acts 27:10) We also, see perception at work in the ministry of Jesus. In Mark 2:8, it reads, "*When Jesus perceived within His spirit.*" Perception can also manifest as a strong desire or an urge to some action. We can again take our example from Jesus in the Gospels.

Jesus was departing Judea and was on His way to Galilee when He

NEEDED to go to Samaria. While at Samaria He meets the woman we know today as the woman at the well (John 4:1-4) Notice how the scriptures read, *"He left Judea and departed again to Galilee. But He needed to go through Samaria."* We can see this principle clearly in this passage.

Sudden Motivation or Inspiration

The other way in which we might experience impressions from God takes the form of motivation and inspiration. We can see this in the scripture as well. The Bible refers to this experience as the stirring of the heart.

We see this idea in the life of Ezra in Ezra 1:5, when he sets out to assist Nehemiah with the rebuilding of the temple. This passage reads, *"...and all whose SPIRITS God had STIRRED..."* In this story we can see that God uses the stirring or motivation of our inner man to lead us in a direction to accomplish his will. I go into great detail about this in the chapter *"The Voice and The Unction."*

We can also see it in other passages such as Acts 17:16 which reads, *"Paul's spirit was provoked within him and he..."* And again in 2 Chronicles 36:22, *"God stirred up the spirit of Cyrus."* Also In Haggai 1:14, *"God inspired the spirits of the men in Haggai to work on the rebuilding of the temple."*

Burdens

The last way that I have found in the scriptures that indicates how God may choose to speak to us is found in Habakkuk 1:1. It reads, *"the BURDEN which the prophet Habakkuk saw"*.

Sometimes God uses our own senses to call our attention to a situation. Habakkuk is in such a situation. God is causing him to see and take notice of the debauchery that is happening around him. What he sees is bothering him. It's bothering him to such a degree that he seeks God about what is happening and God uses this to give him a prophecy.

This is good information for some of you who are trying to find the purpose of God in your life. In a latter book I am writing on how God shows us our destiny, I use this principle to help people to understand why five people can see the same situation of need completely different. It all has to do with the way the Lord directs His burden of vision. Burdens actually combine two or more elements from this chapter. You will experience a perceptual vision and you may perceive what God wants to do through motivation and inspiration. Or you may see a burden and have an experience such as Habakkuk, where Gods speaks to you in an audible voice.

Hopefully the lights are coming on and you are beginning to recognize other times when God was moving in your life by impressions.

Similitudes

The last method that I am going to address regarding this subject is similitudes. A similitude is an analogy or parable. It happens when God takes something natural and makes it relevant to a truth. God can use any number of objects to convey His message. This is probably very common to preachers, who rely on good illustrations to make their points clear.

As I address this subject you will see how perception works to create this experience. In my experience God has blatantly spoken to me in parables using an object to convey His message. At other times He has spoken to me in what I call "perceptual vision".

The Bible says, *"And without a parable He did not speak to them"* (Matt. 13:34, Mark 4:34). This passage refers to how Jesus addressed the many audiences that heard Him speak. Why did He speak in parables? You will find that sometimes the hardest thing to do is to explain a supernatural concept to a natural minded audience. Jesus is having this same problem. He is speaking in reference to the Kingdom of Heaven and the Kingdom of God, and such things as faith and what happens when a demon is cast out to a man. How else could He have explained such abstract concepts to an ordinary people? He used wisdom and decided to use physical elements, which were relevant to the audience. He does so as an attempt to help their understanding of the supernatural realm.

He still speaks this way today. You will see this in the dreams and visions that you will experience. Sometimes the dreams are literal but most of the time they are full of symbolism that the hearer is familiar with or understands.

Just consider my vision above of the sheep that turned into a wolf. He could have shown me the various sins this woman was involved in, but it was much easier and more efficient to just show me an image, which I could relate to from the scriptures.

Later in the chapter on "Signs of His Voice" I tell how God spoke a word to me using He-Man. Yes, He-Man. God used He-Man to teach me the importance of His word and how the Spirit of God empowers us through it. You can read the full account in that chapter, but God will use all sorts of objects to teach you wonderful truths about life and Himself. He knows how to make the complicated easy to understand.

Perceptual Vision

The paragraph above refers to parable similitudes, but what about perceptual vision. Sometimes God will cause you to see an object or situation and then He will inspire you with revelation. We can see this happening in Habakkuk, which we discussed in the last section. He saw something and it became the springboard for revelation. The same thing happened to Jeremiah when God asked him the question what do you see. Then he looked up and saw a boiling pot and it was facing north (Jer.

1:11, 13). He saw something and then God used what he perceived with his eyes to speak to him a prophetic word.

One of the most evident depictions of this is found in Hosea 1:2-4. God tells Hosea to go find a harlot and have children with her. And in obedience Hosea finds a harlot named Gomer and their strained marriage, filled with multiple affairs, becomes a visible representation to communicate Israel's whoring ways. God also uses it to communicate to Israel that even though they break His heart, that He is committed to their union.

Again, Jeremiah 18 shows us a perfect example of this principle. In this chapter Jeremiah is instructed by God to go to the potter's house. While there Jeremiah observes the potter in the process of working with the clay. While observing the potter at work he notices that the clay was spoiled in the hands of the potter. It was so flawed that He made it into another vessel. (see Jer. 18:4)

This observation of the potter interacting with the clay is used as a form of communication with Jeremiah. From the experience God gave birth to a word in Jeremiah. You will see a similar thing happen with a linen loincloth in the thirteenth chapter of Jeremiah.

Ezekiel is another example of this concept. God told him to make a hole in his wall and carry out his belonging through the hole (Ezek. 8:8). He also told him to lie on his side and eat filth (Ezek. 4:4). All this was a visual and dramatic production with one goal I mind. God wanted to communicate a truth.

My children have often been great tools for God to show me truth. I have four beautiful children and our custom at our house is that dessert is only served to those who eat all of their food. One night in particular they were not fond of what mommy had made them for dinner and they were slugging through eating their food. What they did not know was that I had bought something special for them to eat that night, but they would only be able to get it if they ate their food.

I could see that this was not going to end well for them, but I so badly wanted them to have what I had purchased. Suddenly I became aware of the fact that God was saying the same to thing to me. He had a blessing for me and He really wanted to give it to me but He really needed me to make the life adjustments that He required. This is what I call perceptual vision. It is the moment when God causes you to become suddenly aware of some idea He is trying to communicate to you.

All of the information I presented above outlines the ways that God has revealed to me that He speak to us. I know from the many conversations that I have had with people that they have experienced God speaking to them in one of the ways mentioned in this chapter.

Every once in a while, God allows me the privilege of pointing out to people when He is speaking to them. It's always heartwarming for me, and eye opening to them to know that the creator has been trying to get their attention.

Hopefully, the information I presented in this chapter will have the same effect on you. I am also hopeful that it will allow you to come out from among those about whom God says, I speak this way and that way, but man doesn't recognize Me.

About the Author

Kevin Winters is a prophetic minster that has been walking with God for 23 years. His passion is that you know 1) that God is intimate 2) know how to walk in His purpose for your life 3) know how to walk in power, and 4) know how to do spiritual warfare and be victorious. God has gifted him to teach and preach under a prophetic utterance that demonstrates insight and revelation. He is an author, a poet, and a visionary. His ministry is marked by the wisdom and insight that God has given him. God has made him a deep thinker and to most that hear him he is considered a balanced source of revelation.

Currently, Kevin shares God's word through his online ministry. He can be heard weekly on YouTube and Facebook sharing what God is saying and doing in the world in this hour. He also shares his heart in written form by blogging.

By trade he is a visual communication specialist with the Federal Government. In this capacity he serves as a lead graphic designer and illustrator. His hobbies include making music, creating art, martial arts, and enjoying his family.

He resides with Tanya, his wife of 13 years, in Maryland. They have four beautiful children, Autumn, Caleb, Aaron, and Noelle. They are also long time members of the prestigious First Baptist Church of Glenarden where they serve under the leadership of Pastor John K. Jenkins, Sr.

One Last Thing

I would hate to assume that everyone reading this is a Christian. If you are not a believer in Jesus Christ and struggle to understand the concepts of this book, you should know that this is completely normal. The Bible says that unless you are born again you cannot see or understand the things of God.

I would also like to invite you to know what I'm talking about in this book. If you want to meet the God of the Bible then keep reading.

John 3:3
Jesus replied, "Very truly I tell you, no one can see the kingdom of God unless they are born again."

It also says that in order to have the born again experience that one who comes to God must first believe that He is and that He is a rewarder of those who diligently seek Him.

Heb. 11:6
And without faith it is impossible to please God, because anyone who comes to him must believe that he exists and that he rewards those who earnestly seek him.

Your first step toward a brand new life is your acknowledgement of the reality and existence of God. He promises that if you do He will reward you for seeking Him out.

Your next step is to confess with your mouth and believe in your heart that Jesus Christ died on the cross for your sins so that you could enter into a glorious relationship with a welcoming God, who has been waiting for you.

Romans 10:9

If you confess with your mouth that Jesus is Lord and believe in your heart that God raised him from the dead, you will be saved.

Then you need to repent, which simply means to go the other way. Let go of the lifestyle of wickedness and turn towards righteousness. I hear you saying but how?

Acts 3:19

Repent, then, and turn to God, so that your sins may be wiped out, that times of refreshing may come from the Lord,

This is the great part. You do not have to do this on your own. When you accept Jesus as your Lord and Savior He will give you the Helper the Holy Spirit and He will do the job of inspiring in you the very nature of righteousness.

John 15:26

When the Helper comes, whom I will send to you from the Father, that is the Spirit of truth who proceeds from the Father, He will testify about Me, and you will testify also, because you have been with Me from the beginning.

For God imputes or transfers to us His righteousness when we give Him our confessions of nakedness. His Spirit will fill you and empower you to live this life we call Christianity. God made him who had no sin to be sin for us, so that in him we might become the righteousness of God.

2 Corinthians 5:21

God made him who had no sin to be sin for us, so that in him we might become the righteousness of God.

Yes it is that simple. Just say Lord I know I have been wrong and I repent (I am sorry) for the life that I lived. Say Lord, I give you my weakness and my sins and I accept your forgiveness and your righteousness. Confess with your mouth, Lord I believe that Jesus Christ your only begotten Son died on the cross for my sins and was resurrected for me. Then ask Him to fill you with His Spirit and go on with your life living empowered to do right.

If you do not have a church home, then you will need to find one quickly. The Bible tells us that we should be a part of family of like- minded people who can strengthen us and encourage us and help us to grow in the things of God.

Colossians 3:16
Let the word of Christ richly dwell within you, with all wisdom teaching and admonishing one another with psalms and hymns and spiritual songs, singing with thankfulness in your hearts to God.

If you have done all of this, then I would like to say welcome to the family. Now if you read this information again I promise you it will make much more sense. The kingdom of God is not a kingdom that allows one to window shop. You have to come inside to understand it for the Bible says, *"TASTE AND SEE that the Lord is Good"* (Psalm 34:8). You don't get to see until you first taste!

Notes

_____

_____

_____

_____

_____

_____

_____

_____

_____

_____

_____

_____

_____

_____

_____

To hear or read Kevin's teachings visit one of the sites below.

DoinglifeonfFire.org

www.facebook.com/doinglifeonfire

KevinWinters.youtube

Reach out to Kevin

doinglifeonfire@yahoo.com